EXERCISES IN
ENGLISH

grammar

workbook

LEVEL
H

LOYOLA PRESS.

Consultants

Therese Elizabeth Bauer
Martina Anne Erdlen
Anita Patrick Gallagher
Patricia Healey
Irene Kervick
Susan Platt

Linguistics Advisor

Timothy G. Collins
National-Louis University

Editors

Allison Kessel Clark
Beth Renaldi
Ron Watson

Series Design: Loyola Press
Interior Art: Jim Mitchell: 3, 26, 52, 74, 90, 96, 104, 110, 131
All interior illustrations not listed above are ©iStockphoto.com

ISBN-13: 978-0-8294-3642-6; ISBN-10: 0-8294-3642-1

Exercises in English® is a registered trademark of Loyola Press.

Manufactured in the United States of America.

LOYOLA PRESS.
3441 N. Ashland Avenue
Chicago, Illinois 60657
(800) 621-1008
www.loyolapress.com

20 21 22 23 24 25 26 27 LSC 12 11 10 9 8 7 6 5 4

Contents

© Loyola Press. Exercises in English **Level H**

1 Singular Nouns and Plural Nouns

A noun is a name word. A **singular noun** names one person, place, thing, or idea. A **plural noun** names more than one. The plural of most nouns is formed by adding -s or -es to the singular form. For nouns ending in y after a consonant, change the y to i and add -es, such as daisies. Some singular nouns use a different word to show the plural. Some nouns use the same word for the singular and the plural.

A Write the plural form for each noun.

1. ranch _____ranches_____
2. berry _____berries_____
3. mouse _____mice_____
4. barrel _____barrels_____
5. fish _____fish_____

6. journey _____journeys_____
7. class _____classes_____
8. tooth _____teeth_____
9. bus _____busses_____
10. species _____species_____

B Complete each sentence with the plural form of the noun provided.

field

1. Students can work in a number of different _____fields_____ of study in a science lab.

inquiry

2. They have a wide range of tools for their scientific _____inquiries_____.

computer

3. _____Computers_____ are used to tabulate data and to compare results.

change

4. In the lab, students can manipulate _____changes_____ in materials.

series

5. Students can study _____series_____ of changes in physical systems.

process

6. Complicated scientific _____processes_____ can be simulated in a lab.

instrument

7. Students have access to sophisticated _____instruments_____.

dish

8. Biology students can grow cultures in petri _____dishes_____.

microscope

9. They can observe cells with high-powered _____microscopes_____.

technology

10. The _____technologies_____ in labs have improved science education.

2 More Singular Nouns and Plural Nouns

For nouns ending in *o* after a vowel, form the plural by adding *-s* to the singular form. For some nouns ending in *o* after a consonant, form the plural by adding *-es* to the singular. For some nouns ending in *f* or *fe,* change the *f* or *fe* to *v* and add *-es.* For most compound words, form the plural by adding *-s.* For some compounds, make the principal word plural.

A Write the plural form for each noun.

1. sister-in-law _sisters-in-law_
2. potato _potatoes_
3. cell phone _cell phones_
4. leaf _leaves_
5. tie-in _tie-ins_

6. hero _heroes_
7. scarf _scarves_
8. mouthful _mouthfuls_
9. safe _safes_
10. attorney general _attorneys general_

B Complete each sentence with the plural form of the noun provided.

cliff swallow 1. _Cliff swallows_ often live close to people.

gourd 2. Their nests are made of mud and are shaped like _gourds_ .

entrance 3. The _entrances_ to the nests face downward.

cliff 4. The nests are usually built under bridges or on _cliffs_ .

roof 5. Sometimes they are built under the eaves of _roofs_ .

colony 6. Some cliff swallow _colonies_ contain more than 35,000 nests.

mosquito 7. These birds eat flies, _mosquitoes_ , and beetles.

clutch 8. The mother birds lay _clutches_ of three or four eggs.

bull snake 9. Predators such as _bull snakes_ eat many of the eggs.

migrant 10. Every spring these _migrants_ return to San Juan Capistrano.

Name .... Date ....

3 Nouns as Subjects and Subject Complements

A noun can be the subject of a sentence. The **subject** tells whom or what the sentence is about.

Colonists waged war against the British.

A noun that renames or identifies the subject is a **subject complement**. A subject complement follows a linking verb, such as *be* and its various forms (*am, is are, was, were*), *become*, and *remain*.

The war was the beginning of a new nation.

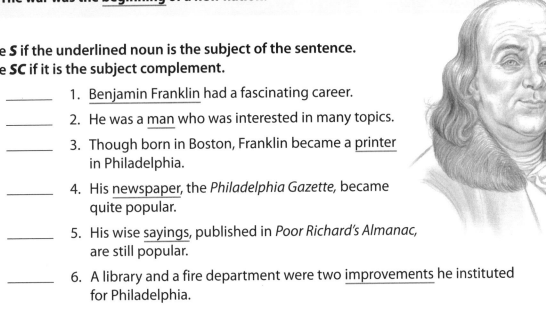

Write *S* if the underlined noun is the subject of the sentence.
Write *SC* if it is the subject complement.

_____ 1. Benjamin Franklin had a fascinating career.

_____ 2. He was a man who was interested in many topics.

_____ 3. Though born in Boston, Franklin became a printer in Philadelphia.

_____ 4. His newspaper, the *Philadelphia Gazette,* became quite popular.

_____ 5. His wise sayings, published in *Poor Richard's Almanac,* are still popular.

_____ 6. A library and a fire department were two improvements he instituted for Philadelphia.

_____ 7. Passionate about exploring unanswered questions, Franklin joined the Leather Apron Club.

_____ 8. By experimenting with a kite, Franklin discovered that electricity and lightning are the same thing.

_____ 9. The Franklin stove was his invention.

_____ 10. Franklin was a deep thinker who became interested in the politics of our young nation.

_____ 11. Franklin was a writer and a signer of the Declaration of Independence.

_____ 12. After the Revolutionary War began, Franklin went abroad to forge an alliance with France.

_____ 13. Many people he met at the French court became his friends.

_____ 14. At the age of 81, Franklin was one of the authors of the U.S. Constitution.

_____ 15. What an interesting life Benjamin Franklin had.

Benjamin Franklin shared his talents by inventing things that helped people in their daily lives and by participating in civic life. Give an example of how you can help others by sharing your talents.

4 Nouns as Objects

A noun can be used as a direct object or an indirect object of a verb or as an object of a preposition. The **direct object** answers the question *whom* or *what* after a verb. The **indirect object** tells *to whom, for whom, to what,* or *for what* the action was done. A noun that follows a preposition in a prepositional phrase is called the **object of the preposition.**

A Underline each noun used as an object. Above each, write *DO* if it is a direct object, *IO* if it is an indirect object, and *OP* if it is the object of a preposition.

1. History gives us many puzzles, such as the disappearance of Amelia Earhart.

2. Even at an early age, Amelia experienced excitement at the thought of flight.

3. Flying offered Amelia unique opportunities with new challenges.

4. She set many records for solo and nonstop flights before she attempted a

   flight around the world.

5. Her tragic disappearance during that trip gives historians a true mystery to solve.

6. Dad's company produces parts for automobiles and for mopeds.

7. Over the years car designers have given customers some great designs.

8. Designers specify the size and other features of each new design.

9. I'm awaiting the arrival of a car with built-in video games and a snack bar.

10. My dream car has fenders that become wings in traffic jams so it can fly.

11. Instruction manuals give buyers information about the operation and care of their cars.

12. When shopping for a car, a person should consider safety features.

13. Many people search the Internet for information on prices and models.

14. Driver education instructors teach students traffic laws and proper driving procedures.

15. Have you seen the announcement about the auto show at the coliseum?

5 Nouns as Object Complements

A noun can be used as an object complement. Just as a subject complement renames the subject, an **object complement** renames the direct object of a verb.

The people elected George W. Bush <u>president</u>.

A If the italicized word is an object complement, write **OC** above it. If it is not an object complement, write **N.**

1. They considered the evening meal a *disaster.*

2. The sun is about 93 million *miles* from Earth.

3. Sharon and Hamad named their daughter *Grace.*

4. Sue calls her floral shop *Love in Bloom.*

5. Christine and Mari completed a 10-mile *hike.*

6. At the memorial service, Arturo gave the first *reading.*

7. In art class the students made black-and-white abstract *drawings.*

8. The organizers of the parade appointed the mayor *grand marshal.*

9. Many Southerners call the Civil War *the War Between the States.*

10. The physics committee named Dr. Ernst Ruska the 1986 Nobel Prize *winner.*

B Use an appropriate noun phrase from Column 2 as an object complement to complete each sentence.

COLUMN 1	COLUMN 2
The school board designated the first Monday in April	the Fun Run
The organizing committee called our fund-raising event	a good sport
Once again the principal named Neil	Activity Day
Because she tries so hard, the other athletes consider May	the official scorekeeper
Neil appointed Harry	chairperson for the event

1. _____

2. _____

3. _____

4. _____

5. _____

6 Appositives

An **appositive** is a word that follows a noun and renames it. An **appositive phrase** is an appositive and its modifiers. A **nonrestrictive appositive** is not necessary in order to understand the sentence; it is set off by commas. A **restrictive appositive** is necessary to understand the sentence; it is not set off by commas.

NONRESTRICTIVE APPOSITIVE	George Washington, our first <u>president</u>, was a surveyor.
RESTRICTIVE APPOSITIVE	The 18th-century printer <u>Parson Weems</u> wrote a biography of George Washington.

A Circle the appositive in each sentence. Underline the noun it renames.

1. Mason Locke Weems, an early historian, was born in Dumfries, Virginia, in 1759.

2. Weems, an Episcopal minister, served as the rector of a parish in Virginia.

3. To support his large family, he became a book agent for Matthew Carey, a Philadelphia publisher.

4. Later he wrote several books, mostly political and moral works.

5. His book *The Life of Washington* tells the tale of George chopping down a cherry tree.

B Identify the appositive in each sentence and decide whether it is restrictive or nonrestrictive. Correct the sentences with nonrestrictive appositives by rewriting them and adding commas where necessary.

1. Phillis Wheatley a girl born in Africa in about 1753 was sold into slavery in 1761.

   _____

2. John Wheatley a prosperous Boston merchant bought her as a servant for his wife.

   _____

3. Phillis a sickly girl was encouraged by the Wheatleys to study literature.

   _____

4. Her book *Poems on Various Subjects* was the first book of poetry ever published by an African American.

   _____

5. John Wheatley emancipated Phillis in 1767, and in 1778 she married John Peters a free black Bostonian.

   _____

   _____

eat

Nouns

W

coat

i

r

larg

eye

big

Name .... Date ....

7 Possessive Nouns

A **possessive noun** expresses possession or ownership. Add -'s to singular nouns and to irregular plural nouns to form possessive nouns.

cat's paws   **women's shoes**

Add only an apostrophe (') to plural nouns that end in s.

students' papers   **hostesses' jobs**

A Write the singular possessive and the plural possessive of each word.

	SINGULAR POSSESSIVE	PLURAL POSSESSIVE
1. child	child's	children's
2. hero	hero's	heroes'
3. man	man's	men's
4. pilot	pilot's	pilots'
5. writer	writer's	writers'
6. secretary	secretary's	secretaries'
7. son-in-law	son-in-law's	sons-in-law's
8. judge	judge's	judges'
9. actress	actress's	actresses'
10. officer	officer's	officers'

B Complete each sentence with the possessive of the noun at the left.

sister-in-law   1. My _sister-in-law's_ watch is very valuable.

David   2. What happened to _David's_ pen?

Mr. Enley   3. _Mr. Enley's_ explanation about the lost items was clear.

police officers   4. The _police officers'_ opinion was different.

men   5. All the _men's_ jewelry was gone.

Sally   6. We looked in the drawer for _Sally's_ silver.

weeks   7. Mr. King donated two _weeks'_ free ad space for the notice.

readers   8. The _readers'_ papers carried news of the thefts.

culprit   9. The _culprit's_ motive was uncovered.

Ms. Alexis   10. _Ms. Alexis's_ detective work paid off.

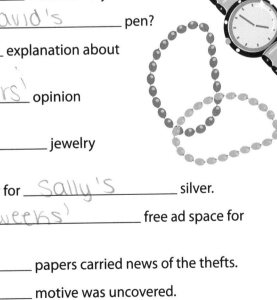

8 Separate and Joint Possession

Separate possession exists when two or more people own things independently of each other. To show separate possession, add -'s to each noun.

John's and Jack's tools

Joint possession exists when two or more people own something together. To show joint possession, add -'s to the last noun only.

John and Jack's hardware store

A Write whether the possessive nouns express separate or joint ownership.

separate 1. Arthur's and Henry's songs were well-performed.

joint 2. It was a good start to North High and South High's art fair.

separate 3. Julia's and Roy's sculptures both used found objects this year.

separate 4. We visited the art exhibit at North's and South's art rooms.

separate 5. Consuela's and her sister's paintings received awards.

separate 6. We always look forward to Jane's and Ann's performances.

joint 7. Tomorrow we will hear Gilbert and Sullivan's opera *The Mikado*.

joint 8. Margo and Anthony's sets really portrayed the mood.

separate 9. A group performed a choral reading of Longfellow's and Whittier's poems.

joint 10. This year awards were given by Thompson and Moreno's Art Emporium.

B For each phrase write a sentence that shows separate ownership.

Rembrandt and Leonardo 1. _____

Jupiter and Saturn 2. _____

Canada and Mexico 3. _____

Sara and Eddie 4. _____

car and truck 5. _____

C For each phrase write a sentence that shows joint ownership.

Mom and Dad 1. _____

Lewis and Clark 2. _____

Jim and Bev 3. _____

Lennon and McCartney 4. _____

freshmen and sophomores 5. _____

9 Reviewing Nouns

A Write **S** if the italicized noun is singular or **P** if it is plural.

_S_   1. Astronomers are discovering much about the *planet.*

_P_   2. We, the *scientists,* are thrilled with the news.

_S_   3. *Mars* might have had life forms.

_P_   4. *Women* have played an important part in space travel.

_P_   5. *Water* has been shown to be trapped between the rocks on Mars.

B Write the plural of each of the following singular nouns.

6. hoof   _hooves_

7. freeman   _freemen_

8. patio   _patios_

9. crossroad   _crossroads_

10. wharf   _wharfs_

11. sheep   _sheep_

12. chocolate chip   _chocolate chips_

13. poppy   _poppies_

14. commander in chief   _commanders..._

15. earful   _earfuls_

C Identify the way each italicized noun is used. Use **S** for subject, **SC** for subject complement, and **APP** for appositive.

_S_   16. At least 50 times a year the *Empire State Building* is struck by lightning.

APP   17. Hippocrates, the *Father of Medicine,* applied logic to medicine.

_SC_   18. A major improvement in health care was the *development* of vaccines.

_S_   19. *Triskaidekaphobia* is the fear of the number 13.

_SC_   20. One major tourist attraction is the *Great Wall of China.*

APP   21. Robinson Crusoe, a marooned *sailor,* was stranded on an island for 28 years.

D Write whether the possessive nouns express separate or joint ownership.

joint   22. Last week we celebrated Joan and Henry's wedding anniversary.

separate   23. Michael's and Dan's gifts were the same.

separate   24. Celia Cruz's and Louis Armstrong's CDs are still popular.

joint   25. We watched Ann and Jack's dance steps at the reception.

Continued →

9

9 Reviewing Nouns, *continued*

E Write the singular possessive and the plural possessive of each word.

	SINGULAR POSSESSIVE	PLURAL POSSESSIVE
26. brother-in-law	_____	_____
27. deer	_____	_____
28. woman	_____	_____
29. hostess	_____	_____
30. goose	_____	_____

F The italicized nouns are used as objects. Write whether each is a direct object **(DO),** an indirect object **(IO),** or the object of a preposition **(OP).**

_____ 31. Henry Ford began his motor *company* in 1903.

_____ 32. He employed 12 workers and made his cars in a *factory.*

_____ 33. Soon Ford ran out of *money.*

_____ 34. A friend's sister gave *Ford* a loan.

_____ 35. Soon many people wanted *Model Ts.*

_____ 36. The company offered *Ford* a way to become wealthy.

G Write whether each italicized noun is used as an appositive **(APP)** or an object complement **(OC).**

_____ 37. The basketball team chose Patrick *captain.*

_____ 38. Have you seen Christie's new horse, *Midnight?*

_____ 39. I cheered for my favorite team, *the Yankees.*

_____ 40. The Bulls called their mascot *Benny.*

Try It Yourself

On a separate sheet of paper, write four sentences about a person or a place. Be sure to use nouns correctly.

Check Your Own Work

Choose a piece of writing from your writing portfolio, a journal, a work in progress, an assignment from another class, or a letter. Revise it, applying the skills you have learned. This checklist will help you.

✔ Have you used the correct spellings of plural nouns?

✔ Have you used nouns in a variety of ways?

✔ Have you used possessive nouns correctly?

© Loyola Press. Exercises in English **Level H**

Name .... Date ....

10 Descriptive Adjectives, Position of Adjectives

A **descriptive adjective** describes a noun's or a pronoun's number, color, size, type, or other qualities.

<u>Beautiful</u> <u>white</u> <u>Austrian</u> horses perform <u>rhythmic</u> movements in the show.

An adjective usually goes before the word it describes. An adjective may, however, follow the word it describes.

The children, <u>eager</u> and <u>excited</u>, waited for a turn to ride the pony.

A Underline the descriptive adjective or adjectives in each sentence.

1. Horses have been useful animals for thousands of years.

2. Before the invention of the car, they were an important means of transportation.

3. Horses' legs, long and muscular, give them the strength to pull heavy loads.

4. Early ancestors of the horse lived in Europe and the Americas.

5. These prehistoric horses had round backs and pointed noses.

6. They were small animals.

7. Modern horses appeared about three million years ago.

8. No one knows when horses became tame animals.

9. Asian peoples used horses in war and for sport thousands of years ago.

10. The disappearance of the prehistoric horse from the Americas has no clear explanation.

B Underline the descriptive adjectives in each sentence. Write **BN** above an adjective if it comes before the noun it describes. Write **AN** if it comes after the noun.

1. Spanish explorers brought horses back to the Americas in the 1500s.

2. New types of horses, Arabian horses, were introduced to Europe in the 1600s.

3. Today's Thoroughbreds, speedy and powerful, are their descendants.

4. Thoroughbreds are the valuable horses that are used for racing.

5. Horses are even participants in Olympic sports.

6. These events feature horses and riders, elegant and sleek.

7. Horses, obedient and responsive, can be trained to follow signals.

8. Good riders know how to make a horse respond to a tiny signal.

9. Horses are generally chosen for a specific purpose.

10. Modern horses vary greatly in size.

© Loyola Press. Exercises in English **Level H**

11 More on the Position of Adjectives

An adjective may come before a noun or after a linking verb. An adjective that follows a linking verb is a **subject complement**.

My teacher is <u>young</u>.

An adjective that follows the direct object and completes the thought expressed by the verb is an **object complement**.

Pretzels make me <u>thirsty</u>.

A **Above each italicized adjective, write _BN_ for before the noun, _SC_ for subject complement, or _OC_ for object complement.**

1. Perhaps you have seen a *small, birdlike* animal at night.

2. It was probably a bat, one of the most *unusual* and *mysterious* creatures.

3. This *swift* creature is actually a *furry* mammal that flies.

4. It sleeps during the day and becomes *active* at night.

5. Contrary to *popular* belief, bats are not *blind*.

6. Most possess *keen* eyesight as well as a *sonar* system.

7. Their ears, which are overly *large,* pick up echoes of the bat's *own* sounds.

8. Despite some *bad* habits, these *birdlike* creatures are *useful*.

9. They make *outdoor* life *bearable* by consuming *great* numbers of insects.

10. Farmers find bats *beneficial* and depend on them to control *harmful* pests.

B **Underline the adjective(s) in each sentence. On the line write _BN_ for before the noun, _SC_ for subject complement, or _OC_ for object complement.**

_____ 1. Valley Forge is a historical park.

_____ 2. It is in southeastern Pennsylvania.

_____ 3. Louis thought the park was fun and informative.

_____ 4. It was important during the Revolutionary War.

_____ 5. The location was strategic.

_____ 6. It could provide many of the basic needs, such as water and wood.

_____ 7. Some of his soldiers found it intolerable.

_____ 8. The weather was severe.

_____ 9. Often the soldiers were cold, hungry, and unfit for service.

_____ 10. It was, however, a turning point for the army.

12 Demonstrative, Interrogative, and Indefinite Adjectives

Demonstrative adjectives point out definite people, places, things, or ideas. The demonstrative adjectives are *this, that, these,* and *those.*

Interrogative adjectives are used in questions. The interrogative adjectives are *what, which,* and *whose. Which* is usually used to ask about one or more of a specific set of items.

Indefinite adjectives refer to any or all members of a group. Indefinite adjectives include *all, another, any, both, each, either, few, many, more, most, much, neither, other, several,* and *some.* Note that *another, each, every, either,* and *neither* are always singular.

A Underline the demonstrative, interrogative, or indefinite adjective in each sentence. Identify each by writing *demonstrative, interrogative,* or *indefinite.*

_____ 1. All fans of jazz music are familiar with the music of Duke Ellington.

_____ 2. What songs by Duke Ellington do you know?

_____ 3. Many people will name songs such as "Mood Indigo" and "Take the A Train."

_____ 4. Few people probably know that his given name was Edward.

_____ 5. Whose idea was it to call him Duke because of his elegant manner?

_____ 6. In the 1920s he did radio broadcasts from New York with his band, and these broadcasts made him famous throughout the country.

_____ 7. Swing and jazz became popular in the 1920s and 1930s, and Ellington was a master of both styles.

_____ 8. Which song is his best?

_____ 9. This question may be answered differently by different fans.

_____ 10. Each fan may have a particular favorite.

B Complete each sentence with the type of adjective indicated.

interrogative 1. _____ CD is on the table?

demonstrative 2. _____ jazz CDs belong to my father.

interrogative 3. _____ instrument do you play in the band?

indefinite 4. _____ people like jazz.

indefinite 5. _____ songs on this CD are by Duke Ellington.

Level H

13 Comparative and Superlative Adjectives

Most adjectives have three degrees of comparison: **positive, comparative,** and **superlative.** For adjectives of one syllable and some adjectives of two syllables, the comparative and superlative are formed by adding *-er* or *-est* to the positive form. For adjectives of three or more syllables and many adjectives of two syllables, the comparative and superlative are formed by adding *more* or *less* or *most* or *least* in front of the positive form.

POSITIVE	COMPARATIVE	SUPERLATIVE
new	newer	newest
sunny	sunnier	sunniest
famous	more/less famous	most/least famous

Some adjectives have irregular comparisons.

POSITIVE	COMPARATIVE	SUPERLATIVE
good	better	best
bad	worse	worst

A Write the comparative and superlative forms of each adjective.

	COMPARATIVE	SUPERLATIVE
1. small	smaller	smallest
2. beautiful	more/less beautiful	most/least beautiful
3. cloudy	cloudier	cloudiest
4. bad	worse	worst
5. delicious	more/less delicious	most/least delicious

B Write the degree of comparison for each italicized adjective. Use **P** for positive degree, **C** for comparative degree, and **S** for superlative degree.

_____ 1. Birds are among the *most interesting* animals.

_____ 2. Some would say that birds are the *most musical* of all animals.

_____ 3. They are *lighter* than most animals because their bones are hollow.

_____ 4. Taking flight is *more difficult* for large birds than for small ones.

_____ 5. One of the *fastest* flying birds is the peregrine falcon.

_____ 6. The ostrich is the world's *most enormous* bird, but it cannot fly.

_____ 7. It is the *speediest* two-legged animal on earth.

_____ 8. Some people think it is *least attractive* of all birds.

_____ 9. The raven may be *smarter* than all other birds since it is very adaptable.

_____ 10. When it cannot find a *favorite* food, it will learn to eat something else.

14 More Comparative and Superlative Adjectives

The comparative degree is used to compare two items or two sets of items. This comparative form is often followed by *than*.

> **Towers such as the CN Tower in Toronto are <u>higher</u> structures than buildings.**

The superlative degree is used to compare three or more items.

> **For many centuries the pyramids were the <u>tallest</u> structures in the world.**

A **Circle the correct choice in parentheses.**

1. The castle of Neuschwanstein is the (more romantic (most romantic)) castle in the world.

2. The (earlier (earliest)) palaces known are in Egypt and were built in the 15th century BC.

3. The Egyptian pyramids, however, are much ((more ancient) most ancient) than those.

4. Some people say that modern buildings are ((less imposing) least imposing) than those old ones.

5. The (taller (tallest)) building in the United States is the Willis Tower in Chicago, at 1,450 feet.

6. At 1,670 feet the Taipei 101 building in Taiwan is ((higher) highest) than the Willis Tower.

7. Some think that the (more unusual (most unusual)) building in the United States is one in the shape of a large duck on Long Island.

8. Do you think that it is ((stranger) strangest) than the Corn Palace in South Dakota, which is decorated with corn and other farm products?

9. Do you think that a duck-shaped building is a (worse (worst)) idea than the binocular-shaped building in Venice, California?

10. Also odd is the Winchester House in California, which has the ((more complicated) most complicated) interior of any house, with staircases that go nowhere.

B **Rewrite the sentences, correcting the errors in the use of the comparative and the superlative degrees.**

1. The most interestingest thing we did in Chicago was to visit the Willis Tower.

   The most interesting thing we did in Chicago...

2. Unfortunately, the day was cloudy, and the view was less clearer than usual.

   ↳ less clear

3. My little brother thought that the view was least exciting than the elevator ride.

   ↳ less exciting

4. The view of the vast lake from above is one of the most magnificentest views you can see.

   ↳ most magnificent

5. Many people think that a visit there is most interesting at night than during the day.

   ↳ more interesting

15 *Few* and *Little* with Concrete Nouns and Abstract Nouns

Concrete nouns name things that you can see, touch, or count. They can be made plural because they can be counted: *minutes, necklaces, chairs.* **Abstract nouns** name things that you cannot see, touch, or count. They express qualities or conditions: *life, patience, time*

Use the adjectives *few, fewer,* and *fewest* to compare concrete nouns. Use the adjectives *little, less,* and *least* to compare abstract nouns.

CONCRETE	**This book on the states has <u>fewer</u> pages.**
ABSTRACT	**That book on the states has <u>less</u> information.**

A Identify each italicized noun as concrete or abstract.

CONCRETE OR
ABSTRACT

1. Mount McKinley is the highest *mountain* in the United States. — concrete

2. Its *height* is 20,321 feet. — concrete

3. *Technology* is an important industry in California. — abstract

4. The *weather* on the Great Plains can be extreme. — abstract

5. It took *determination* to farm that land in the past. — abstract

6. The United States is an important producer of *sugar.* — concrete

7. *Movies* are one of the country's most important exports. — abstract

8. People in the United States drink a lot of *coffee.* — concrete

9. Eight *presidents* were born or lived in Ohio. — concrete

10. *Silver* brought many miners to Nevada in the 1860s. — concrete

B Complete each sentence with *fewer* or *less.*

1. There is _____less_____ rainfall in Utah than in Oregon.

2. Connecticut has _____less_____ land for national parks than Nebraska does.

3. Connecticut also has _____fewer_____ national parks.

4. Alabama produces _____less_____ cotton than Texas does.

5. There are _____fewer_____ farmable acres in Alabama than in Texas.

6. My sister has been to _____fewer_____ parks than I have.

7. Rhode Island has _____fewer_____ landmass than any other state.

8. Wyoming, however, has _____fewer_____ people than Rhode Island has.

9. Lake Erie has _____fewer_____ miles of coastline than Lake Superior.

10. It also contains _____less_____ water.

16 Adjective Phrases

A **prepositional phrase** is made up of a preposition, the object of the preposition, and any modifiers. A prepositional phrase can be used as an adjective. An adjective phrase describes a noun.

A bicycle is a vehicle <u>with two wheels</u>.

A Underline the adjective phrase or phrases in each sentence.

1. The history of the bicycle is a long one.
2. The idea for the modern bicycle did not develop quickly.
3. Cycles with two wheels existed some 200 years ago.
4. The force behind the first bike was not a pedal.
5. The feet of the rider were used to propel the bike and to scoot it along.
6. Bikes from the 1800s did not look like modern bikes.
7. There were bikes with a pedal on the front wheel.
8. The front wheel of some bikes was large, but the back wheel was small.
9. The result of the large front wheel was an increase in the bike's speed.
10. Tires with air were a later addition in the development of the modern bike.

B Underline the adjective phrase or phrases in each sentence. Circle the word each phrase modifies.

1. Bikes for young children have three wheels.
2. Clowns in circuses ride bikes with one wheel.
3. Bicycles with different speeds eventually became popular.
4. The uses of bikes are numerous.
5. Bikes for mountain trails are popular.
6. A feature of mountain bikes is their wide, knobby tires for mountain roads.
7. The challenge of mountain biking attracts many.
8. Today more than 50 million people in the United States cycle regularly.
9. Bicycling is considered a pleasurable form of exercise.
10. Currently more people in China cycle than in the rest of the world together.

17 Adjective Clauses

A **clause** is a group of words that has a subject and a predicate. A dependent clause does not express a complete thought. Some dependent clauses are **adjective clauses.** They describe nouns or pronouns. Adjective clauses are introduced by *who, whom, whose, that, where,* and *when.*

Elizabeth Cady Stanton, <u>who worked tirelessly for women's rights</u>, is an American hero.

A **restrictive** adjective clause is necessary to the meaning of a sentence. A **nonrestrictive** clause is not necessary to the meaning. Nonrestrictive clauses are set off with commas.

The Nineteenth Amendment, <u>which was ratified in 1920</u>, gave women the right to vote.

The amendment <u>that gave women the right to vote</u> was ratified in 1920.

A Underline the adjective clause in each sentence. Circle the noun it modifies.

1. Elizabeth Cady Stanton, who lived from 1815 to 1902, worked for women's suffrage.

2. This movement, which sought to give women the vote, gained momentum in the early 1800s.

3. At the time there were many rights that women did not have.

4. A woman whose husband had died might not be entitled to any of the family property.

5. Many were convinced that the only role that was suitable for women was in the home.

6. Stanton, whose father was a lawyer, became interested in the issue.

7. The women's rights movement was connected to the abolition movement, which was the effort to end slavery.

8. Stanton became acquainted with people who were involved in both movements.

9. Her writings and speeches, which were powerful and eloquent, encouraged others.

10. The year 1878, when Stanton helped prompt Congress to consider an amendment for women's suffrage, marked a key date in her fight.

B Underline the adjective clause in each sentence and decide whether it is restrictive or nonrestrictive. Write the sentences that have nonrestrictive clauses, adding commas where necessary, on the lines below.

1. Stanton who was an outspoken leader gained attention for the cause of women's rights.

   _____

2. The right to vote was just one of the women's rights that Stanton promoted.

   _____

3. Stanton was born in New York where she spent most of her life.

   _____

4. That amendment which gave women the vote was ratified 18 years after her death.

   _____

5. Stanton's determination and energy provide an example for all who fight for rights.

   _____

© Loyola Press. Exercises in English **Level H**

18 Reviewing Adjectives

A Identify the position of each italicized adjective by writing **BN** for before the noun, **SC** for subject complement, or **OC** for object complement.

_____ 1. The *hot, dry* desert has many unusual animals.

_____ 2. Most desert animals are *nocturnal*.

_____ 3. They remain in *underground* burrows during the day.

_____ 4. The animals find the daytime heat *intolerable*.

_____ 5. During the night the temperature is *cooler*.

B Identify each italicized adjective by writing **DES** for descriptive, **DEM** for demonstrative, **IND** for indefinite, or **INT** for interrogative.

_____ 6. John Adams was described as a *political* philosopher.

_____ 7. Before becoming president, he held *many* political positions.

_____ 8. One was the vice presidency, which he termed an *insignificant* office.

_____ 9. In *which* city was he inaugurated?

_____ 10. Philadelphia was the nation's capital at *that* time.

_____ 11. In 1800 he moved into the *damp, unfinished* rooms of the White House.

_____ 12. *Each* year brought new challenges to the *young* country.

_____ 13. His son was elected president *several* decades later.

_____ 14. *That* circumstance has happened only twice.

_____ 15. *What* other families have also produced two presidents?

C Write the comparative and the superlative forms of each adjective.

16. green _____   _____

17. slow _____   _____

18. beautiful _____   _____

19. original _____   _____

20. full _____   _____

Continued →

18 Reviewing Adjectives, *continued*

D Circle the correct adjective in parentheses.

21. The blue whale is the (larger largest) animal that has ever lived.

22. Its body is (bigger biggest) than that of any known dinosaur.

23. The blue whale also makes the (louder loudest) sound of any animal.

24. The female of the species is (more talkative most talkative) than the male.

25. Blue whales, once almost extinct, now exist in (greater greatest) numbers than before.

E Complete each sentence with *fewer* or *less.*

26. If you eat poorly, you will have ___less___ energy.

27. Vegetables have ___fewer___ calories than junk food does.

28. Junk food also provides ___fewer___ vitamins.

29. The ___less___ you exercise, the ___fewer___ calories you will burn.

30. The ___fewer___ junk food you eat, the better you will feel.

F Underline the adjective clause once and the noun it modifies twice. Write on the line whether the clause is restrictive *(R)* or nonrestrictive *(NR).*

_____ 31. A source that can provide up-to-date information is the Internet.

_____ 32. There was a time when most current data came from books and newspapers.

_____ 33. The sites where I found the facts for my essay are all government sites.

_____ 34. Government sites, which are very informative, cover thousands of topics.

_____ 35. Amy, who wrote about the same topic, didn't use the Internet.

Try It Yourself

On a separate sheet of paper, write five sentences that describe an exciting event in your life. Use adjectives correctly.

Check Your Own Work

Choose a piece of writing from your writing portfolio, a journal, a work in progress, an assignment from another class, or a letter. Revise it, applying the skills you have reviewed. This checklist will help you.

✔ Have you included appropriate adjectives?

✔ Have you used the comparative forms of adjectives correctly?

✔ Have you chosen adjectives that create a clear picture for your reader?

19 Personal Pronouns

A **pronoun** is a word that takes the place of a noun. **Personal pronouns** change form depending on **person**—the speaker (first person); the person spoken to (second person); or the person, place, or thing spoken about (third person).

FIRST PERSON	**I, me, mine, we, us, ours**
SECOND PERSON	**you, yours**
THIRD PERSON	**he, she, it, him, her, his, hers, its, them, theirs**

A Underline the personal pronouns in each sentence. Write **1** above each pronoun in the first person, **2** above each pronoun in the second person, and **3** above each pronoun in the third person.

1. Do you enjoy reading fables?

2. They are stories that have a moral or teach a lesson.

3. My sister and I went to the library to look for some fables.

4. We learned that Walt Disney wrote many fables.

5. He told them in comic strips and animated cartoons.

6. Animals played a large part in them.

7. We searched the computer database for other fables.

8. We borrowed books from the library for her and me.

9. In "The Fox and the Lion," a fox is terrified when it meets a lion.

10. You should try to write your own fable.

B Complete each sentence with the correct personal pronoun. The person and the number are given.

Third person, singular   1. The first semester started; ___It___ is the term during which creative writing is taught.

First person, singular   2. The students and ___I___ explored the writing process.

Third person, plural   3. ___They___ would have a good chance of learning about themselves through writing.

First person, plural   4. ___We___ worked to discover new ideas.

First person, plural   5. Working as a team was a worthwhile experience for ___us___ .

20 Personal Pronouns, Number and Gender

A personal pronoun can be singular or plural. The singular pronouns are *I, me, mine, you, yours, he, him, she, her, it, his, hers,* and *its.* The plural pronouns are *we, us, ours, you, yours, they, them,* and *theirs.*

Third person singular personal pronouns also change form, depending on the gender of what is referred to (feminine, masculine, or neuter). The feminine pronouns are *she* and *her;* the masculine pronouns are *he* and *him;* the neuter pronoun is *it.*

A Underline the personal pronoun or pronouns in each sentence. Write **S** (for singular) or **P** (for plural) above each to tell its number. For third person singular pronouns, also write **F** (for feminine), **M** (for masculine), or **N** (for neuter) to tell the gender.

1. Our eighth-grade teacher, Mr. Edwards, gave us a fun assignment last month.

2. He told us that we had to choose a book, read it, and then persuade others to read it.

3. He gave us a list of books, and we had to choose ours by the end of the day.

4. Mine was an action mystery story because that type of book interests me.

5. The main character is Lily; she is determined to be first in the class.

6. She received a B, however, from the social studies teacher, and later he is found dead!

7. Suspicions begin to fall on her, but she knows she is innocent.

8. The book kept me interested, and I knew that it would interest others.

9. I chose a few good passages and read them to the class for my presentation.

10. I asked the other students to tell what they would do in Lily's circumstances.

B Write the correct pronoun for the italicized word or phrase.

_____ 1. Students chose different kinds of books; I enjoyed some of *the other students'.*

_____ 2. *Luisa and I* selected mystery books with school settings.

_____ 3. *Luisa* chose a book by Gordon Korman.

_____ 4. *The book* sounded interesting.

_____ 5. *The hero* is accused of pulling some pranks at school during a play.

_____ 6. *Marcus and Elena* chose books in the Harry Potter series.

_____ 7. I had already read *those books*.

_____ 8. The reports gave *the other students and me* ideas for books to read.

_____ 9. My favorite stories are those in which *students* solve the mysteries.

_____ 10. In one story *a science student* uses his lab equipment to catch a thief.

21 Pronouns as Subjects

A personal pronoun can be used as the subject of a sentence. The **subject pronouns** are *I, we, you, he, she, it,* and *they.*

A Circle the correct pronoun in parentheses.

1. Ellen and (I me) are good friends.
2. (We Us) should help with the packing.
3. My brother and (I me) read an exciting book about winter camping.
4. Have Juan and (him he) returned with the camp stove?
5. Was (he him) given the necessary camping permit?
6. (He Him) and (I me) are partners in the first-aid project.
7. Leo and (him he) quit and joined the rock-climbing class.
8. Neither (he him) nor (she her) has ever been hiking at Starved Rock.
9. (She Her) and her friends have promised to go.
10. Where have Rosa and (she her) put the tents?
11. (We Us) are all going camping this weekend.
12. (Us We) girls have prepared the food pack.
13. You and (me I) will stay in the lodge!
14. (She Her) and (I me) are not going.
15. (We Us) have too much homework.

B On the line write a pronoun that can replace the italicized word or words.

They	1. *The students* began to plan a class trip.
They	2. *Their teacher* suggested going to Washington, D.C.
We	3. "*You and I* will want to see the Air and Space Museum," she said.
He / She	4. *The class secretary* called the bus company.
They	5. *The company* charged $350 for the bus rental.
He	6. *Mr. Zimmerman* gave Sara 75 dollars to spend on the trip.
She	7. *Sara* packed her own snacks to save money for souvenirs.
It	8. *The White House* was the first stop.
They	9. *Dana and Zeke* climbed to the top of the Washington Monument.
It	10. *The trip* was a huge success.

Pronouns

22 Pronouns as Subject Complements

A subject pronoun can be used as a subject complement. A **subject complement** follows a linking verb and refers to the same person or thing as the subject of the sentence.

Mom thought it was I who called.

The pronoun must agree in person (first, second, or third) and number (singular or plural) with the subject. The third person singular must also agree in gender.

A Circle the correct pronoun in parentheses.

1. Was it (she her) who missed the bus?
2. I am not sure if it is (her she).
3. Mr. Fisher said that it could have been (them they).
4. No one would have believed it was (I me).
5. Jim said it was (him he) who called.
6. Cheryl thinks it was (I me) who called her.
7. It isn't (they them) who go to early-morning choir.
8. Mindy could not believe it was (we us) on the bus that early.
9. Last year the route scheduler was (she her).
10. Did you know that the algebra winner was (he him)?

B Complete each sentence with an appropriate pronoun. Write the person, number, and gender of your pronoun on the line at the left.

EXAMPLE:

_____first, pl._____   The first students to enter the hall were _____we_____ .

_____ 1. The buyer of tickets for the entire group was _____ .

_____ 2. The person with the aisle seat is _____ .

_____ 3. The musicians arriving early are _____ , the violinists.

_____ 4. The conductor may be _____ in the gray suit.

_____ 5. A main attraction is _____ , a 10-year-old cellist.

_____ 6. Another performer appearing today will be _____ .

_____ 7. The last soloist to perform is _____ , the vocalist.

_____ 8. Because of your great talent, the soloist should be _____ .

_____ 9. Our music teacher is _____ , sitting in front.

_____ 10. Sometimes a substitute is _____ , the principal.

23 Pronouns as Direct Objects

A personal pronoun can be used as the direct object of a verb. The **object pronouns** are *me, us, you, him, her, it,* and *them.*

The bell startled us.

A **Circle the correct pronoun in parentheses.**

1. Our chemistry teacher surprised (we **us**) last week.

2. The lesson on the periodic table of elements interested (**us** we).

3. The periodic table arranges (they **them**) in rows called periods.

4. Mr. Gonzalez, the teacher, praised Steve and (me **I**) for our report on element 104.

5. The teacher invited (she **her**) to join the chemistry club.

6. All the members wanted (**them** they) on the science team.

7. A science reporter interviewed (he **him**) about the atom model.

8. The newspaper will help (**them** they) with money for more study.

9. The field of chemistry excited (I **me**) after that.

10. The chemistry teacher warned (we **us**) about the work involved.

B **Write the pronoun that correctly replaces the underlined word or words.**

_____him_____ 1. Did you meet Larry at the movie?

_____them_____ 2. Grace invited Steve and Ben to the discussion afterward.

_____us_____ 3. The speaker informed the group and me about movie making.

_____him_____ 4. Have you met Jeremy Black, the *Tribune's* new reviewer?

_____her_____ 5. His opinions sometimes infuriate Sheila.

_____it_____ 6. We saw the movie *Cast Away* on Saturday.

_____us_____ 7. Call Jean and me when you are ready to see it.

_____her_____ 8. After the lecture, Mom expected Mai to come right home.

_____us_____ 9. Instead she joined our friends at the coffee shop.

_____it_____ 10. They criticized the speaker for his latest review.

24 Pronouns as Indirect Objects or as Objects of Prepositions

An object pronoun can be used as the indirect object of a verb.

The secretary read them the minutes.

An object pronoun can be used as the object of a preposition.

The president made copies for her.

A Circle the correct pronoun in each sentence. Write **OP** on the line if it is an object of a preposition or **IO** if it is an indirect object.

_OP_   1. Jan showed (we (us)) her report about Dorothy Day.

_OP_   2. It certainly gave (I (me)) something to think about.

_____   3. One historian referred to (she her) as one of the most significant, interesting, and influential women in America.

_____   4. During the Great Depression, Day established houses of hospitality for less fortunate people; she gave (them they) food, shelter, and hope.

_____   5. The shelters served meals to about 5,000 of (them they) every day.

B Rewrite the following sentences, substituting pronouns for the italicized words.

1. In 1933 Day started a newspaper for Catholic workers with Peter Maurin.

   _____

2. This monthly newspaper gave *the workers* information on peaceful change.

   _____

3. During the 1960s Day showed her support for *activists* by fasting for 10 days.

   _____

4. Mother Teresa gave *Day* a special cross.

   _____

5. My mother handed *my brother* an article about *Dorothy Day*.

   _____

Dorothy Day worked to improve the lives of people who were less fortunate. She spoke out in favor of peace and nonviolent change. Give an example of how you can work for peace and fairness in your daily life.

25 Pronouns After *Than* or *As*

The words *than* and *as* are used in comparisons. These conjunctions often join clauses. Part of the second clause, however, is sometimes omitted. Add the omitted part mentally to determine whether the pronoun needed is a subject pronoun or an object pronoun.

> **Bill is as tall as <u>he</u> (is).** (subject pronoun)
>
> **She takes Wanda to the movies more often than (she takes) <u>me</u>.** (object pronoun)

A   **Circle the pronoun in parentheses with which the italicized word is compared.**

1. In the office *Claire* is as efficient as (she her).

2. The trainer gave *Lanette* fewer pointers on phone use than (me I).

3. *Luce* wrote a more realistic business plan than (he him).

4. Because we took a long break, *we* received our assignment later than (they them).

5. The girls had seen *Keith* more often than (she her) at the copy machine.

6. More computer help-desk requests reach *me* than (he him).

7. The *bosses* are as happy as (we us).

8. *The owners* spend longer hours at work than (they them).

9. Sam offered *Sean* as well as (he him) a full-time job.

10. *Brian* was more excited at the prospect of working than (I me).

B   **Underline the word with which the italicized pronoun is compared.**

1. Christine is older than *I*.

2. Gramps called Ellen more frequently than *her*.

3. My Aunt Jo needed him more than *I*.

4. In the final inning, Johann played better than *he*.

5. Uncle Will threw Josie more curveballs than *me*.

6. Ed told Piku the secret as well as *me*.

7. In the first game, Dad scored better than *I*.

8. Mick gave Ozzie a bigger piece than *me*.

9. Is Jan as short as *she?*

10. Do you know his brother better than *him?*

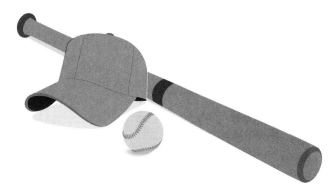

eat
S
W
coat
Pronouns
larg
eye
t
big
r

26 Possessive Pronouns and Adjectives

Possessive pronouns and possessive adjectives show possession or ownership. A **possessive pronoun** takes the place of a possessive noun; it stands alone. The possessive pronouns are *mine, ours, yours, his, hers, its,* and *theirs.*

> **These gloves are Phil's. Here are _mine_.**

A **possessive adjective** modifies a noun and always precedes the noun it modifies. The possessive adjectives are *my, our, your, his, her, its,* and *their.*

> **He said _his_ hands were dirty. [*His* modifies *hands*.]**

A Circle the possessive pronouns. Underline the possessive adjectives.

1. John Greenleaf Whittier spent his boyhood with his parents in Massachusetts.
2. Theirs was a quiet, religious life spent farming.
3. Because his parents were Quakers, Whittier is called the Quaker poet.
4. His poems celebrated our New England country life.
5. His was not just a life spent dreaming about the beauties of rural life.
6. His work against slavery is well known.
7. My history book describes him as an abolitionist.
8. Yours might mention his term in the Massachusetts legislature.
9. Is that copy of "Snow-Bound" ours?
10. I'll give you mine, but you must return it.

B Replace the italicized word(s) with a possessive. Write **A** on the line if the possessive is an adjective or **P** if it is a pronoun.

1. *The Monterey Bay Aquarium's* otters are a popular attraction.
2. Have you read *Roy Nickerson's* book on otters?
3. Much early research into otter behavior was *Dr. Edna Fisher's*.
4. She described many of *the otters'* antics that viewers enjoy.
5. *California's* laws ban the use of gill nets.
6. *A gill net's* victims might include a harbor porpoise.
7. *Tankers' oil spills* are among the greatest dangers.
8. The idea for otter relocation was *a woman's*.
9. Sharks and whales are among *this animal's* natural predators.
10. An otter's need for clean and safe water is like *our need*.

27 Intensive and Reflexive Pronouns

Intensive pronouns and reflexive pronouns end in -self or -selves. An **intensive pronoun** is used to emphasize a preceding noun or pronoun. A **reflexive pronoun** acts as a direct or an indirect object of a verb or as the object of a preposition. A reflexive pronoun refers back to the subject of the clause or sentence.

INTENSIVE   She <u>herself</u> signed the lease.

REFLEXIVE   She informed <u>herself</u> about the terms of the lease.

A Underline the intensive pronoun or the reflexive pronoun in each sentence. Write on the line whether it is intensive **(I)** or reflexive **(R)**.

_____ 1. Bev and Wes themselves chose to do a report on Thomas Edison.

_____ 2. They familiarized themselves with his many achievements.

_____ 3. Bev herself wondered how one person alone could have patented 1,093 inventions.

_____ 4. Wes said that it was possible because Edison never allowed himself to rest.

_____ 5. He added, "Edison himself defined genius as 1 percent inspiration and 99 percent perspiration."

_____ 6. The two decided to reenact Edison's light-bulb experiment for themselves.

_____ 7. They followed the same steps that the inventor himself had followed many years earlier.

_____ 8. They also found that the filament itself was not the only important factor.

_____ 9. After countless attempts and two successful lightings, both students were proud of themselves.

_____ 10. They concluded that Edison's genius spoke for itself.

B Complete each sentence with an intensive pronoun or a reflexive pronoun. If a reflexive pronoun is needed, write **DO** on the line if it is used as a direct object, **IO** if an indirect object, or **OP** if the object of a preposition.

_____ 1. My brother bought a new jigsaw puzzle for _____ .

_____ 2. The puzzle's instruction sheet _____ was hard to figure out.

_____ 3. You _____ are responsible for this puzzle, I told him.

_____ 4. I restrained _____ from putting in even one piece.

_____ 5. Many people buy _____ very challenging puzzles.

Pronouns

28 Agreement of Pronouns and Antecedents

The word to which a pronoun refers is called its **antecedent.** Pronouns agree with their antecedents in person, number, and gender.

<u>Akhenaten</u> (antecedent) **is a source of endless fascination and speculation, but we really know very little about <u>him</u>.**

A **Underline the antecedent for each italicized pronoun. Above the pronoun write *1st, 2nd,* or *3rd* to indicate its person and *S* or *P* for its number. If the antecedent is third person singular, also write *F, M,* or *N* to indicate the gender.**

1. Many mysteries surrounded the discovery of King Tut, and *they* made the boy king famous.

2. Tut ruled for a short time; *he* was the son of the fascinating ruler, Akhenaten.

3. The name of Akhenaten was not included in Egypt's official list of pharaohs, and later people tried to remove *it* from history.

4. One theory is that priests of the popular religion at that time opposed Akhenaten, so *they* wanted to eliminate all traces of him.

5. The Egyptians worshiped many gods, but Akhenaten wanted *them* to worship one god, the sun god Aten.

6. Akhenaten had moved the traditional capital to a different site along the Nile, where *it* now remains a mysterious, desolate place surrounded by desert.

7. In art from the period, Akhenaten and his family are shown worshiping the rays of the sun; *they* are also depicted conducting everyday activities.

8. Nefertiti was one of Akhenaten's wives, and *she* is sometimes pictured with him.

9. The couple were often depicted with long, thin limbs, and *they* had pear-shaped bodies.

10. One sculpture shows Nefertiti with an elegant, swanlike neck, and it has helped establish her as one of history's most beautiful women.

B **Complete each sentence with the appropriate pronoun or pronouns. Make sure that each agrees with its antecedent in person, number, and gender.**

1. Scientists continue to look for artifacts related to Akhenaten in hopes that _____ will find more clues to the mysteries surrounding _____ .

2. The art of Akhenaten's time indicated a huge break from the style of earlier Egyptian monarchs, and _____ undoubtedly shocked his subjects.

3. Akhenaten encouraged changes in building methods also. _____ included such things as smaller stone blocks set in strong mortar.

4. After Akhenaten died, his city was abandoned, and _____ crumbled over time.

5. The temples were torn down, and stones from _____ were used in other buildings.

Pronouns

29 Agreement of Intensive Pronouns and Reflexive Pronouns

Intensive pronouns and reflexive pronouns must agree with their antecedents in person, number, and gender.

A Circle the intensive pronoun or the reflexive pronoun in each sentence. Write *1st, 2nd,* or *3rd* on the line at the left to indicate person and *S* or *P* to indicate number of the antecedent. If the pronoun is third person singular, also write *F, M,* or *N* to indicate its gender.

_____ 1. Did you hurt yourself when you fell?

_____ 2. We made ourselves comfortable in the boat.

_____ 3. I myself find little that is new in the navigation course.

_____ 4. He has no confidence in himself.

_____ 5. Jean herself completed the work on her small sailboat.

_____ 6. My sister herself cooked lunch in the boat's microwave.

_____ 7. You should prepare yourself for a storm on Monday.

_____ 8. She herself lost courage after that last outing.

_____ 9. She blamed nobody but herself for the tragedy.

_____ 10. Suddenly we found ourselves in a beautiful harbor.

B Rewrite each sentence, adding an intensive pronoun or a reflexive pronoun. Add additional words as necessary. Write *I* on the line at the left if the addition is intensive or *R* if it is reflexive.

_____ 1. Martin Luther King Jr. and other African American civil rights leaders found a place in history.

_____

_____

_____ 2. Martin Luther King Jr. was jailed for his nonviolent protests.

_____

_____

_____ 3. King's supporters were often the targets of violence.

_____

_____ 4. I recently read King's "I Have a Dream" speech.

_____

_____ 5. The work for civil rights was carried on by Coretta Scott King.

_____

Pronouns

30 Interrogative Pronouns

An **interrogative pronoun** is used to ask a question. *Who, whom,* and *whose* are used when asking about people. *Who* is used when the pronoun is the subject of the question. *Whom* is used when the pronoun is the direct object or indirect object of the verb or the object of a preposition. *Whose* is used when asking about possession. *Which* is used when asking about one member of a class or group of persons, places, or things. *What* is used for asking about things and seeking information.

A Underline the interrogative pronouns. Write on the line whether each pronoun seeks information about a person, place, or thing.

_____ 1. Who has driven along the coast of California?

_____ 2. What are some of the sights we can see?

_____ 3. What should you take for the climate changes?

_____ 4. Which is the best park to visit in Big Sur?

_____ 5. My mother asked, "Which of the authors lived on Cannery Row?"

_____ 6. Who wants to go to the aquarium?

_____ 7. Which of the state parks has the elephant seals?

_____ 8. For whom was Hearst Castle named?

_____ 9. Who is worried about driving on Highway 1?

_____ 10. To which of the attractions do you wish to travel?

B Circle the interrogative pronoun in each sentence. Write on the line whether it is used as the subject **(S)**, the subject complement **(SC)**, the direct object **(DO)**, the indirect object **(IO)**, or the object of a preposition **(OP)**.

_____ 1. Which of Edison's inventions is most important?

_____ 2. Who was Jan Matzeliger?

_____ 3. Who invented the traffic light?

_____ 4. To whom is industry indebted for the automatic lubricator?

_____ 5. Which of the problems faced by farmers in the West did Glidden solve?

_____ 6. Mrs. Swenson gave whom the report on Baekland's important new material?

_____ 7. Who discovered electricity?

_____ 8. What do you wish to invent, Natalie?

_____ 9. In which of the references did you find information on Margaret Knight?

_____ 10. Whom do you admire?

31 Interrogative Pronouns *Who* and *Whom*

Who is used as a subject pronoun in questions as the subject or subject complement. *Whom* is used as an object pronoun as the direct object or indirect object of the verb or as the object of a preposition.

A Circle the interrogative pronoun in each sentence. On the line at the left, write what its role is in the sentence—*S* for subject, *SC* for subject complement, *DO* for direct object, *IO* for indirect object, or *OP* for object of a preposition.

_____ 1. Who directed the 1981 Academy Award–winning *Chariots of Fire?*

_____ 2. To whom did Dorothy turn for help in *The Wizard of Oz?*

_____ 3. Who wrote the poems mentioned in the movie *Il Postino?*

_____ 4. Who was the lead actor in *Forrest Gump?*

_____ 5. By whom was the Ark of the Covenant stolen in the first Indiana Jones movie?

_____ 6. Shostakovich gave whom permission to use his musical score?

_____ 7. Whom did you meet at the Oscar party?

_____ 8. Who owned the small bookshop in *You've Got Mail?*

_____ 9. Who was the oldest person to win an Oscar?

_____ 10. Whom did you see at the movies last night?

B Complete each sentence with *who* or *whom*.

1. _____ was chained to a cliff to be devoured by a monster but was instead rescued by Perseus?

2. _____ slew the Minotaur and married Ariadne?

3. With _____ did the nymph Echo fall in love?

4. _____ did Zeus kill for driving the sun chariot too close to the earth?

5. _____ did Paris carry to Troy, an act that led to the Trojan War?

6. _____ was the Queen of Heaven and the wife of Zeus?

7. _____ unwittingly murdered his father and married his mother?

8. By _____ was Medusa, the gorgon, slain?

9. After _____ have we named our books of maps?

10. _____ threw himself into the Aegean Sea in distress?

Pronouns

32 Demonstrative Pronouns

A **demonstrative pronoun** points out a specific person, place, or thing. Use *this* and *these* to point out things that are near. Use *that* and *those* to point out things that are farther away. *This* and *that* are singular. *These* and *those* are plural.

A Circle the demonstrative pronoun in each sentence. Write whether it indicates near or distant objects.

_____ 1. This is the painting you wanted to see.

_____ 2. Look at the brush strokes and notice how these are close together.

_____ 3. This is a painting far superior to the one in the brochure.

_____ 4. Those are among the paintings in the gallery on the second floor.

_____ 5. The curator is happy that you brought these in today.

_____ 6. Do you like this?

_____ 7. Those are similar to woodcuts we saw last year in Europe.

_____ 8. Unfortunately, that was the trip we had to cut short.

_____ 9. This was painted by Rembrandt in his early years.

_____ 10. These are unusual frames.

B Complete each sentence with the correct demonstrative pronoun.

1. The softest pillows are _____ on this couch.

2. Is _____ your car at the end of the driveway?

3. _____ is the first time I have seen the recipe.

4. _____ are the only pieces left in this box.

5. _____ in the next room are from the Ming dynasty.

6. Was _____ your brother on the bus?

7. The only change I could find is _____ in my pocket.

8. Mother's flowers are _____ at our feet.

9. _____ are my friends standing on the next corner.

10. What is _____ rising over the mountain?

© Loyola Press. Exercises in English **Level H**

33 Relative Pronouns

A relative clause is a dependent clause that describes or gives information about a noun.

A **relative pronoun** joins the dependent clause to its antecedent in the main clause. The relative pronouns are *who, whom, whose, which,* and *that. Who, whom,* and *whose* refer to people. *Which* refers to places or things. *That* refers to people, places, or things.

Hal (antecedent), **who** (relative pronoun) **grew up in Indonesia, lives in Chicago.**

A Underline the relative pronoun in each sentence. Circle its antecedent.

1. Mountains are landforms that are higher than their surroundings.

2. The mountain that you climb may be a hill to someone else.

3. The Alps, which are considered a young mountain range, are a mere 15 million years old.

4. Sir Edmund Hillary, who became the first person to climb Mount Everest, did so in 1953.

5. Tenzing Norgay was the Sherpa guide who accompanied Hillary.

6. Other climbers whom you may have read about have also accomplished the feat.

7. Mount Whitney, which is in the Sierra Nevada range, is the highest mountain in California.

8. Ararat, which is in Turkey, is where Noah's Ark is said to have ended up after the great flood.

9. Mountain climbers, whose journals are often published, can have interesting tales to tell.

10. *Into Thin Air,* which chronicled one climb, was quite popular.

B Underline the relative pronoun in each sentence. Write on the line whether it is a subject or an object and how it is used in the sentence.

EXAMPLE:

subject of <u>is outstanding</u>   **The Newberry Library has a collection of maps that is outstanding.**

_____   1. Maps are tools that are used by travelers and students.

_____   2. A map that shows the surface of the earth is called a physical map.

_____   3. Road maps, upon which I depend for my job, are designed for travelers.

_____   4. Scale, from which a user can determine real distance, is an important map feature.

_____   5. A globe is a map that is mounted on a ball.

Pronouns

34 *Who* and *Whom* as Relative Pronouns

The relative pronoun *who* is used when the pronoun is the subject of the relative clause.

The girl who entered the room was Carrie.

The relative pronoun *whom* is used when the pronoun is the direct object or indirect object or the object of a preposition in the relative clause.

The first person whom we will visit is Uncle Dan.

A Circle the correct relative pronoun in parentheses. Write on the line whether it is a subject or an object and how it is used in the sentence.

_____ 1. The young woman (who whom) you met is Augusta Reed Thomas, composer-in-residence.

_____ 2. Bach was a composer (who whom) has received much study.

_____ 3. Mozart is the composer (who whom) I favor.

_____ 4. He is the one (who whom) wrote *The Magic Flute*.

_____ 5. Was it Beethoven (who whom) composed *Fidelio*?

B Complete each sentence with a dependent clause that contains the relative pronoun **who.**

1. The singer, _____ , performs once each year.

2. Her accompanist, _____ , plays in a jazz group.

3. Another artist, _____ , lives in our building.

4. At a Chicago hotel, I saw Stevie Wonder, _____ .

5. I work for the conductor, _____ .

C Complete each sentence with a dependent clause that contains the relative pronoun **whom.**

1. Have you seen the oboist, _____ ?

2. Hugh, _____ , wanted to see an opera.

3. Dr. Yurkanin, _____ , telephoned for tickets.

4. I wrote a thank-you note to Francesca, _____ .

5. The diva, _____ , was a joy to hear.

35 Indefinite Pronouns

An **indefinite pronoun** refers to any or all members of a group of people, places, or things. Some common indefinite pronouns are *all, another, both, each, either, few, many, neither, nothing, several, some,* and pronouns that begin with *any* or *every.*

Each must pass the physical.

Anyone who is qualified can join.

A Underline the indefinite pronouns.

1. One of the officials blew a whistle, and each of the windsurfers paddled out to sea.

2. Today was the windsurfing race, and everybody was on the beach.

3. The brisk wind quickly filled all of the sails.

4. After about 10 seconds, several of the surfers stood up on their boards.

5. A few headed to the south, and many went to the southeast.

6. An official said that either of the routes would be fast because of the strong wind.

7. After an hour someone caught sight of two sails on the horizon.

8. Neither was close enough, so it was impossible for anyone to tell who was in the lead.

9. As the boats neared, both seemed to be the same distance from shore.

10. Somebody said that this would be a photo finish!

B Underline the indefinite pronouns. Identify the role each plays in the sentence. Write **S** for subject, **SC** for subject complement, **DO** for direct object, **IO** for indirect object, or **OP** for object of a preposition.

_____ 1. Has anybody ever attended a focus group?

_____ 2. The company sent each of us an invitation.

_____ 3. After the introduction everybody tasted the cheese spreads.

_____ 4. One woman found none of them satisfactory.

_____ 5. After the first test, the moderator introduced another.

_____ 6. Did the moderator give you both of the yogurts to try?

_____ 7. Cheese, yogurt, and ice cream are a few of my favorite foods.

_____ 8. She gave each of us a rating sheet to complete.

_____ 9. I received curious looks from a few of the reviewers.

_____ 10. Neither of the reviewers next to me wanted to fill out the form.

36 Agreement with Indefinite Pronouns

An indefinite pronoun refers to any or all of a group of people, places, or things. Some indefinite pronouns are always singular; others are always plural; and some can be either singular or plural.

SINGULAR	**anyone, anybody, anything, each, either, neither, everyone, everybody, everything, one, no one, nobody, nothing**
PLURAL	**both, few, many, others, several**
SINGULAR OR PLURAL	**all, any, more, most, none, some**

A Circle the correct word in parentheses. Underline its antecedent.

1. Each of the women was satisfied with (her their) booth at the bazaar.

2. Neither of the food booths had (its their) food ready in time.

3. Many of the guests did not park (her their) cars in the lot.

4. All of the people showed up for (his their) free movie passes.

5. Everyone on the boys' team explained (his their) part of the project.

B Complete each sentence with an appropriate pronoun or possessive adjective. The pronouns and adjectives must agree in person with the italicized word.

1. If *anybody* wishes to study earthquakes, _____ can start now.

2. *Both* of my sisters liked _____ earth science classes.

3. *Everyone* is expected to do _____ own lab assignments.

4. *Many* of the students have read _____ assignments already.

5. A *few* of the students dropped _____ science courses this semester.

6. *Each* had _____ volcano model evaluated by an expert.

7. Has *anyone* completed _____ seismograph project?

8. *Neither* of the seismologists admitted that _____ had missed the warning signs.

9. *Several* of the new students wondered if _____ had the right teachers.

10. Generally, *all* of the students are satisfied with _____ courses.

37 Reviewing Pronouns

A **Circle the correct pronoun in parentheses. Identify the role each plays in the sentence. Write S for subject, SC for subject complement, DO for direct object, IO for indirect object, or OP for object of a preposition.**

_____ 1. It was (they them) who invited us to the party.

_____ 2. Charlie made a celebratory lunch for (her she).

_____ 3. He plans to send Maria and (she her) the leftovers.

_____ 4. Charlie and (me I) planned the surprise months ago.

_____ 5. Could (us we) keep it a secret?

_____ 6. Charlie kept the plans with (he him) in his journal.

_____ 7. Sunday we finally told (her she).

B **Underline the reflexive pronoun or intensive pronoun in each sentence. Write R if it is reflexive or I if it is intensive.**

_____ 8. I myself knew his voice when I heard it.

_____ 9. She looked at herself in the mirror.

_____ 10. The twins made the iced tea for themselves.

_____ 11. He himself told me the story.

C **Underline the pronoun in each sentence. Write whether the pronoun is demonstrative, indefinite, possessive, or interrogative.**

_____ 12. That was the movie I saw last week.

_____ 13. Sam noted that each of the actors wore black.

_____ 14. The movie gave neither a fair portrayal.

_____ 15. What is the kind of story that makes the best screenplay?

_____ 16. Someone once said real-life dramas make the best movies.

_____ 17. That opinion isn't mine.

Continued →

37 Reviewing Pronouns, *continued*

D Complete each sentence with *who* or *whom*.

18. _____ wrote *The Maltese Falcon?*

19. To _____ was the starring role given?

20. _____ did Sydney Greenstreet play in the movie?

21. Do you know _____ played opposite Humphrey Bogart?

E Circle the correct pronoun following *than* or *as*.

22. Jenny is as excited as (she her) about the car trip.

23. George has planned his vacation more carefully than (they them).

24. My dad liked the Yellowstone campsite better than (he him).

25. Bridget didn't care as much as (we us).

26. Fran complained more than (me I).

F Circle the correct possessive adjective in parentheses.

27. Either of my brothers will give you (his their) baseball glove.

28. Neither of my sisters remembered (her their) workout clothes.

29. Each of the girls on the track team wore (her their) own sweat pants.

30. Several of the girls' parents offered (his their) help to buy uniforms.

Try It Yourself

On a separate sheet of paper, write four sentences about something you treasure. Be sure to use pronouns correctly.

Check Your Own Work

Choose a selection from your writing portfolio, a journal, a work in progress, an assignment from another class, or a letter. Revise it, applying the skills you have reviewed. This checklist will help you.

✔ Have you remembered to make pronouns and their antecedents agree?

✔ Have you used subject pronouns and object pronouns correctly?

38 Principal Parts of Verbs

A **verb** expresses action or a state of being. The **principal parts** of a verb are the **base form,** the **present participle,** the **past,** and the **past participle.** The present participle is formed by adding *-ing* to the base form. The past and past participles of regular verbs are formed by adding *-d* or *-ed* to the base form. The past and past participles of irregular verbs are not formed by adding *-d* or *-ed* to the base form.

BASE	PRESENT PARTICIPLE	PAST	PAST PARTICIPLE
sharpen	sharpening	sharpened	sharpened
eat	eating	ate	eaten
go	going	went	gone

A Write the past and the past participle of each verb. Then write whether the verb is regular or irregular.

	PAST	PAST PARTICIPLE	
1. wait	_____	_____	_____
2. catch	_____	_____	_____
3. choose	_____	_____	_____
4. return	_____	_____	_____
5. miss	_____	_____	_____
6. steal	_____	_____	_____
7. get	_____	_____	_____
8. haunt	_____	_____	_____
9. feel	_____	_____	_____
10. forget	_____	_____	_____

B Complete each sentence with the past or the past participle of the verb provided.

read   1. Have you ever _____ any of Aesop's fables?

tell   2. People have _____ fables for centuries to teach useful lessons.

feel   3. Aesop _____ that his humorous writings would help people.

hide   4. Writers generally _____ the lessons in fables.

write   5. Aesop _____ a story about a lion.

represent 6. In the story the lion _____ the king.

grow   7. The lion _____ old and could not hunt for food.

come   8. When visitors _____ to see him, he ate them.

choose   9. The fox had _____ not to visit the lion.

come   10. The fox realized the other animals had not _____ out of the lion's den.

39 Transitive Verbs and Intransitive Verbs

A **transitive verb** expresses an action that passes from a doer to a receiver. The receiver of the action is the direct object.

> **Frost killed the flowers.**

An **intransitive verb** has no receiver of the action. It does not have a direct object.

> **The flowers died.**

A Underline the verb or verb phrase in each sentence. If the verb is transitive, write **T** on the line and circle the receiver of the action. If it is intransitive, write **I.**

_____ 1. In the early 1800s, passenger pigeons numbered in the billions.

_____ 2. Their flocks once darkened the skies.

_____ 3. Less than 100 years later, they no longer existed in the wild.

_____ 4. Many factors caused the bird's extinction.

_____ 5. Hunting, trapping, and loss of habitat each played a role.

_____ 6. The pigeons lived in the eastern United States and Canada.

_____ 7. Settlers used pigeons as a source of meat.

_____ 8. Their feathers make pillows and mattresses.

_____ 9. Passenger pigeon populations dwindled.

_____ 10. By 1880 their numbers declined irreversibly.

_____ 11. Scientists bred the birds unsuccessfully in captivity.

_____ 12. Nothing could prevent their extinction.

_____ 13. The last passenger pigeon died in captivity in 1914.

_____ 14. Today, extinction is threatening many other species.

_____ 15. The fate of the passenger pigeon teaches a valuable lesson.

B Some verbs may be either transitive or intransitive depending on how they are used. Write **T** if the italicized verb is transitive and **I** if it is intransitive.

_____ 1. Sandy sat on the porch and _read_ all afternoon.

_____ 2. Ken _read_ "Jack and the Beanstalk" to the twins.

_____ 3. Today the Cooking Club _baked,_ roasted, and broiled.

_____ 4. I _baked_ Tom's birthday cake myself.

_____ 5. We _rode_ along the lakefront bike path.

40 Troublesome Verbs

The following pairs of verbs are easy to confuse. Learning the meaning of each word is the best way to avoid mistakes.

Teach (taught, taught) means "to give knowledge."
Learn (learned, learned) means "to receive knowledge."

Take (took, taken) means "to carry from a near place to a more distant place."
Bring (brought, brought) means "to carry from a distant place to a near place."

Lend (lent, lent) means "to let someone use something of yours."
Borrow (borrowed, borrowed) means "to take something and use it as one's own with the idea of returning it."

Lie (lay, lain) means "to recline."   **Lay (laid, laid) means "to place."**

Sit (sat, sat) means "to take a seat."   **Set (set, set) means "to put down."**

Rise (rose, risen) means "to get up."   **Raise (raised, raised) means "to lift up."**

A **Circle the correct verb in each sentence.**

1. Dorothy (rises raises) before sunrise every morning.
2. I would never (take bring) my camera into the pool.
3. Would you (bring take) my book over here when you come?
4. Every experience (learns teaches) us a lesson.
5. Charlene (borrowed lent) me her tent when I went camping.
6. Lamont (sat set) the pie on the counter after he baked it.
7. The hot air balloon (rose raised) above the treetops.
8. We can't all (sit set) at one table in the cafeteria.
9. Lou (raised rose) the flag as the parade passed by.
10. Karen (lies lays) on the sofa for half an hour every afternoon to watch TV.

B **Complete each sentence with the correct form of the verb.**

set   1. The older students _____ a good example for the younger ones.

lay   2. Maz _____ his books on the table after he got home from school.

lie   3. They have _____ there ever since.

lie   4. The cat had _____ on the sunny porch all day.

take   5. The teacher asked, "Who has _____ Lenny's pencil?"

lend   6. I know you _____ me a dollar last week, but I am still broke.

teach   7. Regina has _____ her sister to play chess.

raise   8. Camille _____ her hand because she knew the answer.

rise   9. Johann _____ slowly after the bruising tackle.

bring   10. When Isabelle went to the bakery, she _____ me back a Danish.

41 Linking Verbs

A **linking verb** joins the subject with a subject complement, which may be a noun, a pronoun, or an adjective.

NOUN	PRONOUN	ADJECTIVE
Washington <u>was</u> president.	It <u>is</u> she.	I <u>became</u> hungry.

A Circle the linking verb in each sentence. Underline the subject complement. Write above the complement whether it is a noun (N) or an adjective (ADJ).

1. Most folk songs are ballads that tell simple stories.

2. Many of these songs are an expression of political or religious beliefs.

3. The composers of these songs often remain anonymous.

4. As the songs are passed to new generations, the melodies often become simpler.

5. In many songs the verses are a story, and a chorus is sung between them.

6. The guitar is the most popular instrument used by folksingers today.

7. Many folk songs were work songs.

8. Other folk songs became simple entertainment.

9. Singers today feel sympathetic toward social concerns.

10. As enjoyment, folk music remains popular in many countries.

B Complete each sentence with an appropriate linking verb.

1. An opera _____ a drama set to music.

2. The texts of operas _____ sung.

3. Martin _____ an opera singer last year.

4. He _____ one of the lead singers in the school musical.

5. As he _____ older, his voice may get deeper.

6. Right now his voice _____ very high and clear.

7. He gets excited when he _____ the star of the show.

8. With his costume on, he _____ much older.

9. Martin's favorite composer _____ Mozart.

10. Mozart _____ a composer at the age of six.

42 Active Voice and Passive Voice

A transitive verb can be in the active voice or the passive voice. When in the **active voice,** the subject is the doer of the action. When in the **passive voice,** the subject is the receiver of the action.

John Hancock <u>signed</u> the Declaration of Independence.

The Declaration of Independence <u>was signed</u> by John Hancock.

Underline the verb in each sentence. Write _A_ on the line if it is in the active voice or _P_ if it is in the passive voice.

_____ 1. A million tons of chocolate will be consumed in the United States this year.

_____ 2. Much of this chocolate is produced by the Hershey Company.

_____ 3. In 1872, at age 15, Milton Hershey started a candy-making apprenticeship.

_____ 4. By 1886 he had founded a successful caramel company.

_____ 5. A second company was soon created.

_____ 6. This new company produced only chocolate.

_____ 7. The business was located in Derry Church, Pennsylvania.

_____ 8. Milton Hershey had been born there.

_____ 9. The factory was completed in 1905.

_____ 10. An affluent community quickly grew around the factory.

_____ 11. A year later the town was renamed Hershey.

_____ 12. Milton Hershey believed that advertising was unethical.

_____ 13. His factory was opened to the public.

_____ 14. The company's products were promoted through word of mouth.

_____ 15. Hershey donated much of his time and money to the town.

_____ 16. In 1909 Hershey established a school for orphans.

_____ 17. The school was endowed with stock from his company.

_____ 18. The school originally was spread over several miles.

_____ 19. The Hershey Company employed many of the school's graduates.

_____ 20. Today Hershey produces many well-known candies.

Verbs

43 Simple Tenses

Verb forms indicate **tense,** or the time of the action. The **simple present tense** tells about an action that is repeated or that is always true. The **simple past tense** tells about an action or a condition that happened in the past. The **simple future tense** tells about an action or a condition that will happen in the future.

PRESENT	PAST	FUTURE
I <u>eat</u> hot dogs.	I <u>ate</u> a hot dog last night.	I <u>will eat</u> a hot dog for lunch tomorrow.

A Underline the verb in each sentence. Write its tense on the line.

_____ 1. The human body contains more than 600 muscles.

_____ 2. Scientists discovered three kinds of muscles in the body.

_____ 3. These are the skeletal, the smooth, and the cardiac muscles.

_____ 4. The cardiac muscles are located only in the heart.

_____ 5. The skeletal muscles hold the skeleton together.

_____ 6. Smooth muscles are found in the organs of the body.

_____ 7. These muscles control the body processes.

_____ 8. Muscle functions will stop under certain conditions.

_____ 9. Sudden muscular contractions caused severe muscle cramps in many athletes.

_____ 10. After repeated exercise and work, your muscles will be capable of strenuous work.

B Complete each sentence with the correct form of the verb provided.

grow–*past* 1. Last summer Serena _____ a vegetable garden.

eat–*past* 2. She _____ fresh vegetables every day.

be–*present* 3. Vegetables _____ the edible products of herbaceous plants.

contain–*present* 4. Vegetables _____ many nutrients.

water–*past* 5. Serena _____ the plants each morning.

hope–*present* 6. She _____ to have a garden again next year.

plant–*past* 7. Last year she _____ carrots, potatoes, and squash.

add–*future* 8. Next summer she _____ tomatoes and peppers.

be–*present* 9. Tomatoes and peppers _____ actually fruit.

help–*future* 10. Her grandfather _____ her plant the seeds.

44 Progressive Tenses

Progressive tenses express continuing action. The progressive tenses consist of a form of the auxiliary verb *be* and the present participle of the main verb. The **present progressive tense** tells about something that is happening right now.

> **The Tower of Pisa is leaning.**

The **past progressive tense** tells about something that was happening in the past.

> **It was leaning many years ago.**

The **future progressive tense** tells about something that will be happening in the future.

> **Engineers will be trying to stop it from leaning farther.**

The **perfect progressive tenses** tell about things that happen over time.

PRESENT	**I have been working in the garden all day.**
PAST	**She had been working there for years when she heard the news.**

A **Complete each sentence with the progressive form of the verb.**

study–*present perfect* 1. Scientists _____ the Galapagos Islands for many years.

observe–*past* 2. Charles Darwin _____ the islands in 1835.

work–*past perfect* 3. He _____ as a naturalist on the *HMS Beagle*.

find–*past* 4. He _____ many unique species on the islands.

take–*future* 5. Students _____ notes during their field trips.

B **Underline the progressive verb phrase in each sentence. Write its tense on the line.**

_____ 1. Today humans are causing many problems for the Galapagos Islands.

_____ 2. The Galapagos tortoises had been living without natural predators.

_____ 3. By the 16th century, humans were visiting the islands.

_____ 4. Pirates and whalers were butchering the tortoises for food.

_____ 5. Settlers were also introducing foreign species to the ecosystem.

_____ 6. These new species are endangering the tortoises.

_____ 7. Dogs brought by settlers are attacking the defenseless animals.

_____ 8. Goats are eating the plants that tortoises once fed on.

_____ 9. Until they are removed, goats will be stripping away the vegetation.

_____ 10. Environmentalists are trying to preserve the Galapagos tortoise.

Verbs

45 Perfect Tenses

The **perfect tenses** consist of a form of the auxiliary verb *have* and the past participle of the main verb. The **present perfect tense** tells about an action that took place at an indefinite time in the past and continues into the present. The **past perfect tense** tells about a past action that happened before another past action. The **future perfect tense** tells about an action that will be completed before a specific time in the future.

PRESENT PERFECT	**I have eaten breakfast.**
PAST PERFECT	**I had eaten before I left for school.**
FUTURE PERFECT	**I will have eaten breakfast by that time.**

Progressive forms of the perfect tense indicate ongoing actions: I have been working (*present perfect progressive*), I had been working (*past perfect progressive*), I will have been working (*future perfect progressive*).

A Underline the verb in each sentence. Write its tense on the line.

_____ 1. It has been more than a century since Theodore Roosevelt succeeded William McKinley as president.

_____ 2. Roosevelt had been serving as McKinley's vice president.

_____ 3. After only six months into McKinley's second term, however, someone had assassinated him.

_____ 4. At 42, Roosevelt had become the youngest president ever.

_____ 5. In 1905 he had been negotiating a treaty for the Russo-Japanese War.

_____ 6. Earlier he had named the Grand Canyon a national monument.

_____ 7. The government has preserved the park since 1893.

_____ 8. Millions of tourists will have visited the park by December.

_____ 9. Roosevelt's conservation policies have influenced many generations of conservationists.

_____ 10. He has remained one of our most colorful presidents.

B Complete each sentence with form of the verb indicated.

remain–*present perfect*

1. Charlie Chaplin _____ popular for nearly a century.

study–*present perfect progressive*

2. We _____ his films in our history class.

star–*past perfect*

3. By 1957 he _____ in more than 70 films.

see–*present perfect*

4. Our teacher _____ every one of his movies.

watch–*future perfect*

5. We _____ *City Lights* and one other Chaplin film by tomorrow.

46 Indicative Mood and Imperative Mood

Verb forms also indicate *mood*. The **indicative mood** is the form of a verb used to state a fact or ask a question.

> **Scrapbooking is becoming more and more popular.**
> **What is scrapbooking?**

The **imperative mood** is the form of a verb that is used to give commands.

> **Learn more about this popular hobby and craft.**

A Underline the verb or verb phrase in each sentence. Write **IN** to identify verbs in the indicative mood or **IM** to identify verbs in the imperative mood.

_____ 1. Why do people do scrapbooking?

_____ 2. Guess the reasons.

_____ 3. People use a scrapbook as a storage place for information about many things in their lives, such as trips, school events, and parties.

_____ 4. Think of something in your life to use as a scrapbook topic.

_____ 5. What things do you find in a scrapbook?

_____ 6. Scrapbooks usually include photos as well as small objects or souvenirs, such as tickets and programs.

_____ 7. List other possible contents for your scrapbook.

_____ 8. An important feature of scrapbooking is journaling.

_____ 9. What is journaling?

_____ 10. People describe the objects in the scrapbook in captions or blocks of text.

_____ 11. Look for examples of scrapbooks online.

_____ 12. Some people use the computer as a tool in scrapbooking.

_____ 13. They even create scrapbook pages on the computer as Web pages.

_____ 14. Have you seen any of these?

_____ 15. Take a look at these often beautifully styled pages.

B Rewrite each sentence in the imperative mood. Add or delete words as necessary.

1. First you should choose an event or a theme, such as a school picnic or a hobby.

_____

2. It is important to find the best photos of the event.

_____

3. You need to get supplies such as paper, scissors, glue, and an album.

_____

4. Creating a sample page layout is essential.

_____

5. You should try to be creative and use your artistic sense.

_____

47 Subjunctive Mood

The **subjunctive mood** of a verb can express a wish or a desire or a condition that is contrary to fact. Present wishes or desires or contrary-to-fact conditions are expressed by the past tense. *Were* is used with all subjects.

WISH OR DESIRE	**I wish I were going to the movie with you.**
CONTRARY TO FACT	**If he were caught up with all his chores, he could go.**

Past wishes, desires, or contrary-to-fact conditions are expressed by the past perfect tense.

WISH OR DESIRE	**I wished I had read the assignment.**
CONTRARY TO FACT	**If I had read it beforehand, I would have had all the answers.**

The subjunctive is also used to express a demand or a recommendation after *that, if,* or *whether.* The base form is used for these subjunctive verbs.

Her teacher recommended that she take singing lessons.

A Underline the verb or verb phrase in the subjunctive mood in each sentence. On each line at the left, write *W* to identify a wish or a desire, *C* to identify a contrary-to-fact condition, or *D* to identify a demand or recommendation.

_____ 1. I wish I had a mountain bike.

_____ 2. If I had more money, I would buy one.

_____ 3. If I had saved money, I would have been able to get one.

_____ 4. I wish I hadn't spent so much money on my school trip.

_____ 5. If I had had a bike last year, I would have had more fun on our vacation at the lake.

_____ 6. If I were the owner of one, I would be able to travel all around the lake area.

_____ 7. My mother recommends that I get a part-time job.

_____ 8. She insists, however, that I take piano lessons one day a week.

_____ 9. She also suggests that I be a member of the choir.

_____ 10. My friend says, "If I were you, I'd try to find work caring for people's yards."

B Circle the correct verb to complete each sentence in the subjunctive.

1. The experts recommend that a potential bike owner (go goes) to a local shop.

2. So if I (was were) buying a mountain bike, I would go to a local shop and look at the models available.

3. If I (was were) you, I would buy a model from the previous year because they are usually less expensive.

4. Safety advisors insist that every biker (get gets) a crash helmet.

5. We wish that there (was were) a place to rent mountain bikes near here.

48 Modal Auxiliaries

Modal auxiliaries are used to express permission, possibility, ability, necessity, obligation, or intention. They are used with main verbs in the base form. Common modal auxiliaries are *may, might, can, could, must, should, will,* and *would.*

> **All citizens may exercise their right to vote.** (permission)
> **In some countries, citizens must vote.** (necessity)

The passive voice is formed by inserting *be, have been,* or *had been* between the modal auxiliary and the past participle.

> **Special elections may be held on special issues.** (possibility)

A Underline the verb phrase with a modal auxiliary. Tell if the modal auxiliary expresses permission, possibility, ability, necessity, obligation, or intention. More than one description may be possible for some sentences.

_____ 1. In a democracy, voters can decide on their leaders.

_____ 2. In Australia every eligible citizen must register for the vote.

_____ 3. People in the United States may register if they choose to do so.

_____ 4. Every citizen should vote in elections.

_____ 5. Any U.S. citizen 18 years old or older may participate in an election.

_____ 6. The Twenty-Sixth Amendment says that 18-year-olds may vote.

_____ 7. At one time only adult white males could vote.

_____ 8. Now citizens of all races and genders may vote.

_____ 9. Although the Fifteenth Amendment says that people of all races could vote, many African Americans were denied this right for years.

_____ 10. You should read about the history of the struggle for women's suffrage.

_____ 11. My older brother will vote for the first time in the next election.

_____ 12. People who are not at home on election day may cast absentee ballots.

_____ 13. Your life may be affected by the new elected leaders.

_____ 14. For example, the amount of money in the budget for education and libraries might be decided by them.

_____ 15. People should take their duty to vote seriously.

B Complete each sentence with a verb phrase containing a modal auxiliary. Use the main verb and the meaning of the modal shown in parentheses. More than one answer may be correct for some sentences.

1. People born in other countries _____ U.S. citizens. (become–*permission*)

2. Applicants for citizenship _____ 18 years old. (be–*necessity*)

3. They _____ in the United States for five years. (have lived–*necessity*)

4. They _____ to the principles of the U.S. Constitution. (agree–*obligation*)

5. They _____ a test to show that they know basic facts about the U.S. government. (take–*necessity*)

49 Subject-Verb Agreement

A verb always agrees with its subject in person and number. The only verbs that need to change form to agree with their subjects are the verb *be* and verbs in the present tense with third person singular subjects.

The man <u>rides</u> a bicycle.

The men <u>ride</u> bicycles.

Sometimes a phrase comes between the subject and the verb. The verb must agree with the subject, not the phrase.

The dog, like many other pets, <u>gets</u> fleas.

A meal of potatoes and hot dogs <u>is</u> filling.

A Complete each sentence with the correct form of the present tense of the verb provided.

bring　　1. Olympic events __bring__ together the world's finest athletes.

bear　　2. Couriers __bear__ a lighted torch from the valley of Olympia, Greece.

carry　　3. The final runner __carries__ the torch into the stadium.

light　　4. Here the runner __light__ the Olympic flame to open the games.

burn　　5. This flame __burns__ until the end of the Games.

B Circle the correct form of the verb in parentheses.

1. The 1936 Olympic competition, held in Berlin, ((was) were) emotionally tense.

2. Imagine that the year is 1936, and Adolf Hitler (lead (leads)) Germany.

3. Hitler, the leader of the Nazis, (want (wants)) his athletes to win.

4. Jesse Owens, however, ((is) are) the star of the Olympics.

5. Owens, among the first African American U.S. Olympians, (win (wins)) three solo gold medals.

6. He and his other team members also ((triumph) triumphs) in the 100-meter relay.

7. Owens and the other Americans ((shatter) shatters) the Nazi leader's hopes.

8. The image of Owens decorated with four gold medals ((was) were) an inspiration to persecuted people everywhere.

9. After the Olympics, Owens ((was) were) active in youth athletic programs.

10. Owens, one of the world's great athletes, ((remains) remain) a source of inspiration.

Jesse Owens inspired people everywhere with his courage and determination. What inspires you? Write about how another person has inspired you.

50 *Doesn't* and *Don't*

Doesn't is used when the subject of the sentence is third person singular.

- **Lucy doesn't care.**

Don't is used with other subjects.

I don't care.   **We don't care.**

You don't care.   **Lucy's friends don't care.**

A **Circle the correct form of the verb in parentheses.**

1. I (doesn't **don't**) remember who she is.

2. Most Americans (doesn't **don't**) work on Labor Day.

3. Why (**doesn't** don't) Anita drink her tea while it's hot?

4. My mother (**doesn't** don't) want me to stay up late.

5. We (doesn't **don't**) have a blender.

6. Nina (**doesn't** don't) have to practice on Saturday.

7. You (doesn't **don't**) need to read Chapter 7.

8. Mr. Esposito (**doesn't** don't) have any children.

9. (**Doesn't** Don't) Jerry know he shouldn't wear his hat inside the house?

10. Those three dogs (doesn't **don't**) belong to Randy.

B **Complete each sentence with *doesn't* or *don't*.**

1. A rainbow _doesn't_ always appear after it rains.

2. Carmen _doesn't_ have enough time to see a movie.

3. We _don't_ want to spend our vacation in Antarctica.

4. Sid realized he _doesn't_ look like Abraham Lincoln.

5. The security guard _doesn't_ allow anyone in after six.

6. We _don't_ care if she has ever played baseball before.

7. _Don't_ you have any homework tonight?

8. Tina and Harriet _don't_ want to miss the concert.

9. The dress _doesn't_ have to be blue.

10. I _don't_ want to miss tomorrow's football game.

Verbs

51 *There Is* and *There Are*

When *there is* or *there are* introduces a sentence, the subject follows the verb. Use *there is (was, has been)* with singular subjects. Use *there are (were, have been)* with plural subjects.

There <u>are</u> about 50 million <u>tourists</u> to Italy every year.

A **Circle the correct verb form in parentheses.**

1. There (is **are**) many tourist attractions in Italy.
2. In Florence alone there (is **are**) many magnificent works of art.
3. During the 1400s there (**was** were) a revival of learning known as the Renaissance.
4. There (was **were**) important Renaissance artists from Florence, including Leonardo da Vinci and Michelangelo.
5. There (was **were**) interest at that time in the writings of the ancient Greeks and Romans.
6. There (**is** are) a famous museum in Florence called the Uffizi Gallery.
7. There (**was** were) once Michelangelo's original statue of David in a nearby piazza, but it is now in a museum.
8. There (**is** are) still, however, a copy of the imposing work in the piazza.
9. There (**is** are) one landmark in Rome that is the main symbol of the city—the Colosseum.
10. There (**was** were) entertainment in that arena during the time of the ancient Romans.
11. There (**was** were) once many ancient roads connecting places within the Roman Empire.
12. Throughout Europe there (is **are**) still traces of the old roads.
13. There (is **are**) many fairs in Italian towns throughout the year.
14. There (is are), for example, celebrations that feature local products and foods, including artichokes, asparagus, pepperoni, and gnocchi (a kind of dumpling).
15. Down the center of Italy there (is are) a mountain chain.
16. There (is **are**) the Alps in the north.
17. There (is are) also active volcanoes in Italy, including Mount Vesuvius and Mount Etna.
18. Many people know there (was were) a big eruption of Mount Vesuvius in AD 79.
19. There (has been have been), however, other eruptions of that volcano throughout history.
20. There recently (has been have been) concern over the deterioration of famous landmarks such as the Leaning Tower of Pisa.

B **Complete each sentence with *is* or *are*.**

1. There _____ a famous horse race in Siena, Italy.
2. There _____ horses representing the city's various *contrade,* or sections, in the race.
3. There _____ strong rivalry among these historic sections.
4. There _____ often plots to stop a rival from winning the race.
5. There _____ a prize for winning—a banner called the *Palio.*

52 Agreement with Compound Subjects

Compound subjects connected by *and* usually require a plural verb. If, however, the subjects connected by *and* refer to the same person, place, or thing, or express a single idea, the subject is considered singular.

Chickens and ducks <u>are</u> both poultry.

Ham and eggs <u>is</u> my favorite breakfast.

A **Circle the correct form of the verb in parentheses.**

1. Rock and roll (is are) a style of music that originated in America in the 1950s.

2. Many adults and children (was were) shocked by this new form of music.

3. Jazz and country music (was were) incorporated into rock and roll.

4. Rhythm and blues (is are) also considered a main influence.

5. Bill Haley and the Comets (was were) one of the first successful acts.

6. "Shake, Rattle, and Roll" (was were) probably the group's biggest hit.

7. Chuck Berry and Fats Domino (was were) also popular singers.

8. The most famous singer and performer (was were) Elvis Presley.

9. This musician and actor (remain remains) popular today.

10. *Frankie and Johnny* (is are) just one of the movies that Elvis starred in.

B **Complete each sentence with *is* or *are.***

1. Macaroni and cheese _____ a popular side dish.

2. Macaroni and cheese _____ the two main ingredients in the casserole.

3. "To serve and protect" _____ the motto of our police department.

4. Serving and protecting _____ worthy goals of any police officer.

5. Fox and Geese _____ an old children's game.

6. The fox and the geese _____ making a ruckus in the barnyard.

7. *Bob and Ray* _____ an old radio program inducted into the Radio Hall of Fame.

8. Bob and Ray _____ living legends in the history of radio.

9. Stars and stripes _____ painted all over Jessica's toy chest.

10. _____ "Stars and Stripes" going to be played at the veterans' ceremony?

53 Agreement with Compound Subjects Connected by *Or* or *Nor*

When a compound subject is joined by *or* or *nor,* the verb agrees with the subject closer to it.

Neither the dog nor the <u>cats</u> <u>are</u> inside.

Neither the cats nor the <u>dog</u> <u>is</u> inside.

A Circle the correct form of the verb in parentheses.

1. Neither the lunch nor the dinner (come comes) with dessert.

2. (Was Were) either Muriel or Pedro at the wedding?

3. Neither he nor I (work works) on Sunday.

4. Either Mr. Anderson or you (is are) responsible.

5. Neither the gas bill nor the electric bill (was were) mailed on time.

6. Either my grandparents or my father (pick picks) me up from school.

7. Neither the horse's feet nor its legs (was were) injured in the accident.

8. Neither the pillows nor the mattress (arrive arrives) today.

9. Either Logan or I (has have) to babysit Veronica.

10. Neither the teacher nor the students (know knows) who will be selected.

B Complete each sentence with the correct form of the present tense of the verb provided.

is   1. Either the tuna or the mayonnaise _____ rancid.

watch 2. Neither he nor I _____ television on weeknights.

is   3. Neither Madeline nor her friends _____ going to the meeting.

feed   4. Either Walter or his daughters _____ the fish when I am away.

read   5. Neither the man nor his wife _____ the newspaper.

like   6. Neither you nor my brother _____ taking tests.

walk   7. Either Homer or I _____ the dog before school.

match 8. Either the hat or the gloves _____ her coat.

smell 9. Neither the trainer nor his animals _____ bad.

know   10. Neither the players nor their coach _____ how to get to the stadium.

54 Agreement with Subjects Preceded by *Each*, *Every*, *Many a*, or *No*

When two or more subjects connected by *and* are preceded by *each, every, many a,* or *no,* the subject is considered singular.

A **Circle the correct form of the verb in parentheses.**

1. Every man, woman, and child (has have) heard of Bigfoot.

2. Each report and piece of evidence (feed feeds) the public's imagination.

3. The Himalayan Yeti and the Canadian Sasquatch each (fit fits) the description.

4. No culture or society (is are) without some form of this legend.

5. Each Russian folktale, Greek myth, and Anglo-Saxon fable (has have) a similar figure.

6. Many a scientist and investigator (doubt doubts) the existence of Bigfoot.

7. Each photograph and sighting (is are) examined.

8. Every bird and mammal (leave leaves) some trace behind.

9. A family says every story and report (was were) false.

10. They say each footprint and sound attributed to Bigfoot (was were) created by a family member.

B **Complete each sentence with the correct form of the present tense of the verb provided.**

has   1. Many a clam and oyster _____ been found in that bay.

is   2. Every mother and father _____ coming to the play.

walk   3. Each student and teacher _____ outside when the alarm bell rings.

show   4. Every boy and girl here _____ signs of improvement.

is   5. At the airport every bag and box _____ inspected.

has   6. Each football team and soccer team _____ a pep rally.

bring   7. Every friend and relative _____ a present.

has   8. No child or adult _____ received a ticket to the fair.

need   9. Each lion and tiger _____ a separate cage.

read   10. Many a teacher and student _____ the school paper.

Verbs

55 Agreement with Indefinite Pronouns

The indefinite pronouns *each, either, neither, one, anyone, no one, anybody, nobody, someone,* and *somebody* are always singular.

Each lives in an apartment. Nobody lives in a house.

A Underline the subject in each sentence. Circle the correct form of the verb in parentheses.

1. Everyone in Basil and Manuel's class (is are) going on a field trip.

2. Neither of the boys (has have) turned in his permission slip.

3. Everyone in the class (get gets) to see the Guggenheim Museum.

4. Anyone without a permission slip (is are) not allowed to go.

5. Each of the students (receive receives) a reminder.

6. No one (want wants) to miss this trip.

7. One of the 20th century's greatest architects (is are) the museum's designer.

8. Everyone in the class (know knows) that Frank Lloyd Wright designed it.

9. Each of his designs (remain remains) influential.

10. Anyone visiting the museum (know knows) it is a work of art in itself.

B Underline the subject in each sentence. Complete each sentence with the correct form of the present tense of the verb provided.

play	1.	Nobody _____ as well as Diego.
bring	2.	Someone _____ Maria the newspaper every day.
be	3.	Neither of the dogs _____ tired of playing.
ride	4.	In Europe nearly everyone _____ a bicycle.
prepare	5.	Someone different _____ dinner each night.
goes	6.	On the night before a test, everybody _____ to bed early.
know	7.	Anyone _____ where that building is located.
need	8.	One of these cakes _____ icing.
appear	9.	Nobody _____ to have watered the vegetables.
want	10.	No one _____ to drink water from that pond.

Verbs

56 Agreement with Collective Nouns

A **collective noun** names a group of people or things: *audience, team, litter*. A collective noun is generally thought of as a single unit and takes a singular verb. However, when the meaning suggests that the members are being considered as individuals, use a plural verb.

The football team <u>practices</u> indoors when it rains.

The football team <u>are</u> responsible for their own uniforms.

A Circle the correct form of the verb in parentheses.

1. The choir (is are) not back from its concert tour to New England and Canada.

2. The faculty (was were) debating all sides of the issue.

3. The faculty (was were) unanimous in its decision.

4. The French club (meet meets) in the library after school on Wednesday.

5. The jury (has have) been selected by the attorneys.

6. His family (is are) currently living in Florida and Georgia.

7. Congress (was were) in session all week.

8. The flock of birds (flies fly) north after the summer ends.

9. The team (was were) operating as smoothly as a Swiss watch.

10. The audience (have has) taken their seats, and now the concert is about to begin.

B Write sentences, using the collective noun given as the subject.

club 1. _____

team 2. _____

herd 3. _____

band 4. _____

group 5. _____

57 Agreement with Special Nouns

Some nouns are plural in form but singular in meaning. Among these are *measles, mathematics, mumps, news, ethics, physics,* and *economics.* Each of these nouns requires a verb that agrees with a singular subject.

The news is terrible.

Some nouns are used only in the plural; for example, *ashes, clothes, eaves, goods, pincers, pliers, proceeds, scissors, shears, suspenders, glasses, scales, thanks, tongs, trousers,* and *tweezers.* Each of these nouns requires a verb that agrees with a plural subject.

Thanks are in order.

A **Underline the subject in each sentence. Circle the correct verb in parentheses.**

1. The tweezers (go goes) in the medicine cabinet.

2. Economics (is are) sometimes taught in high school.

3. The ashes from the fireplace (have has) not been removed.

4. The garden shears (make makes) the job a lot easier.

5. The eaves on the guest house (was were) painted last summer.

6. Bernadette's clothes (give gives) her a formal appearance.

7. Diego's suspenders (keep keeps) his pants from falling down.

8. News (spread spreads) quickly in this modern electronic age.

9. The proceeds from the bake sale (was were) used to buy new uniforms.

10. Abby's glasses (need needs) to be fixed.

B **Complete each sentence with *is* or *are.***

1. The pliers _____ in the toolbox.

2. Safety scissors _____ better for young children.

3. Civics _____ an interesting and important subject for children to study.

4. Rupert's slacks _____ made out of linen.

5. Mumps _____ a contagious disease.

6. Thanks _____ due to our parents for their kindness and support.

7. Those rusty tongs _____ of no use to anyone.

8. Mathematics _____ Dejuan's favorite subject.

9. Emma's clothes _____ in need of ironing.

10. The news _____ coming on at six.

58 Reviewing Verbs

A   **Underline the verb in each sentence. On the first line, write _T_ if the verb is transitive or _I_ if it is intransitive. On the second line, write _A_ if the verb is active or _P_ if it is passive.**

_____   _____   1. Some animals migrate every year.

_____   _____   2. Monarch butterflies are found in Canada and the United States in the summer and in Mexico in the winter.

_____   _____   3. Many birds fly to new homes every spring and fall.

_____   _____   4. Pacific salmon complete their migration over their lifetimes.

_____   _____   5. These migratory patterns are studied by U.S. and Canadian scientists

B   **Underline the linking verb in each sentence. Circle the subject complement.**

6. Irruption is an unpredictable form of migration.

7. Lemmings are an example of an animal that migrates in this manner.

8. Another migratory pattern is remigration, which occurs across generations.

9. Many scientists are intent on studying irruption.

10. Animal migration is hard for scientists to track.

C   **Complete each sentence with the correct form of the verb provided.**

study–*present progressive, active*

11. June's class _____ animal migration.

taught–*present perfect, passive*

12. It _____ many interesting facts.

visit–*future, active*

13. The students _____ the Columbia River next semester.

migrate–*future progressive, active*

14. The Chinook salmon _____ then.

travels–*present, active*

15. This salmon _____ more than 2,000 miles to spawn.

place–*present perfect, passive*

16. These fish _____ on the threatened-species list.

hatch–*present, active*

17. Baby salmon _____ in rivers and streams.

swim–*future, active*

18. After spending their adult lives in the ocean, they _____ back to the same river to spawn.

58 Reviewing Verbs, *continued*

prevent–*present perfect, active*

19. Dams across the rivers _____ some salmon from reaching their spawning grounds.

work–*present perfect progressive, active* 20. Many people _____ to save the salmon.

D Write on the line the mood of the italicized verb. Use **A** for indicative, **B** for imperative, and **C** for subjunctive.

_____ 21. *Return* these books to the library.

_____ 22. Lamont wishes he *were* already on vacation.

_____ 23. My sister *is reading* a scary book.

_____ 24. If Emily *were* here, she would know what to do.

_____ 25. Nathan *can walk* to school if he chooses.

E Circle the correct verb in parentheses.

26. The team (is are) meeting before the game.

27. The team (has have) to win to advance in the tournament.

28. Each of the players (want wants) to do well.

29. Neither of the captains (know knows) which team is playing today.

30. After the game was over, everyone (raised rose) to leave.

Try It Yourself

On a separate sheet of paper write five sentences about something you and your friends do together. Be sure to use verbs correctly.

Check Your Own Work

Choose a selection from your writing portfolio, a journal, a work in progress, an assignment from another class, or a letter. Revise it, applying the skills you have reviewed. This checklist will help you.

✔ Have you conveyed the meaning clearly and accurately by using the correct forms of the verbs?

✔ Have you written the correct form of any troublesome verbs?

✔ Have you used verb tense correctly?

59 Participles

A **participle** is a verb form that is used as an adjective; it can be used to modify a noun or a pronoun. Present participles end in *-ing,* and past participles often end in *-ed.*

> **The cat <u>chasing</u> the mouse grew tired.** (present participle)
>
> **The mouse, <u>chased</u> by the cat, ran into a small hole.** (past participle)

Underline the participle used as an adjective in each sentence. Identify the tense of each by writing *present* or *past* on the line at the left.

_____ 1. Walking at night, Kay often sees meteors.

_____ 2. Streaking across the sky, they are a magnificent sight.

_____ 3. Brilliant meteors, known as fireballs, are quite dramatic.

_____ 4. Some, called bolides, have even been observed to explode like thunder.

_____ 5. A meteor reaching a planet in one piece is called a meteorite.

_____ 6. Kay, listening in class, learned that comets break up and form meteors.

_____ 7. Asteroids and comets are small solid objects orbiting the sun.

_____ 8. Three of the largest asteroids—called Ceres, Pallas, and Vesta—are found in a single asteroid belt.

_____ 9. Located between Mars and Jupiter, they do not pose a threat to Earth.

_____ 10. A giant asteroid may once have hit Earth, striking the Yucatan Peninsula.

_____ 11. The Yucatan, located in Mexico, is marked by a giant crater.

_____ 12. Coinciding with the dinosaurs' disappearance, that collision is believed to have killed them off.

_____ 13. What other theories offered by scientists explain their disappearance?

_____ 14. One, proposed by a health researcher, suggests that a fungus may be to blame.

_____ 15. He theorizes that fungi attacked their bodies, causing sickness and death.

Verbals

60 Placement of Participles

A participle used as an adjective is called a **participial adjective.** It can come before or after the noun it modifies or after a linking verb.

Do not cry over spilled milk.

The crumbs lying on the floor need to be swept up.

His meal was very nourishing.

A Underline the participial adjective in each sentence. Circle the word it modifies.

1. The icicle, melting rapidly, fell from the gutter.

2. It is dangerous to drive fast on the winding road.

3. The news, blaring from the TV, caught my attention.

4. It is important to watch for falling rocks while climbing.

5. The battle of Gettysburg was a turning point in the Civil War.

6. The dog growling in the yard scared off the hoodlums.

7. Simon had only one misspelled word in his paper.

8. We must repair that broken window.

9. The figure at Mabel's door was disturbing.

10. Chan threw out the chipped plate.

11. The baby chick emerged from the cracked egg.

12. The branches of the willow, swaying gracefully in the breeze, were a lovely sight.

13. The sound of running water attracted the deer to the river's edge.

14. As we listened, the story became more exciting.

15. The written word is an important link to the past.

B Use each phrase in a sentence. Underline each participle. Circle the noun it modifies.

raging storm   1. _____

retired athlete   2. _____

purring cat   3. _____

freezing rain   4. _____

known facts   5. _____

61 Dangling Participles

A participle that does not modify any noun or pronoun in the sentence is called a **dangling participle**.
Avoid these in your writing.

DANGLING	**Working for days, the paper was completed.**
	(*Working* does not modify a noun.)
CORRECTED	**Working for days, the student completed the paper.**
	(*Working* modifies *student*)

A   Write **C** to the left of each sentence in which the participle is used correctly.
Underline the participle and circle the word it modifies.

_____   1. Sitting at the table, we were served pancakes and milk.

_____   Sitting at the table, pancakes and milk were served.

_____   2. Walking along the beach, there was a beautiful sunset.

_____   Walking along the beach, I saw a beautiful sunset.

_____   3. Nursing an injury, the performance was terrible.

_____   Nursing an injury, the dancer performed terribly.

_____   4. Lacking the money, John did not buy the bicycle.

_____   Lacking the money, the bicycle remained unpurchased.

_____   5. Having eaten ice cream already, the lunch remained untouched.

_____   Having eaten ice cream already, Eve left her lunch untouched.

B   Rewrite the following sentences to avoid the dangling participle.

1. Climbing out of the pool, the beach chair came into view.

   _____

2. Reaching into the refrigerator, the milk was taken out.

   _____

3. Reading all night, the book was finished.

   _____

4. Jogging early in the morning, the cool breeze is refreshing.

   _____

5. Standing at the chalkboard, the lesson was presented by the teacher.

   _____

Verbals

62 Gerunds as Subjects

A **gerund** is a verb form ending in *-ing* that is used as a noun. A gerund may be used as the subject of a sentence. A **gerund phrase** may include a direct object and modifiers.

>   **Exercising** is good for your health. (gerund)

>   **Keeping a strict routine** can be difficult. (gerund phrase with a direct object)

A   Underline the gerund phrase. Draw an additional line under the gerund.

1. Catching fish is fun.

2. Baiting the hook is not as much fun.

3. Threading a worm on a hook requires patience.

4. Selecting a flashy lure may help catch some types of fish.

5. Making lures with exotic feathers is a popular hobby.

6. For some people, rowing the boat is the most fun.

7. Being outside is enough for others.

8. For my father, chasing a record catch is the goal.

9. Cooking and eating the fish are my mother's favorite part.

10. Identifying the fish is as close as I want to get.

B   Write sentences, using the gerund or gerund phrase as the subject.

walking around the track	1. _____
exercising	2. _____
drinking water	3. _____
listening	4. _____
eating balanced meals	5. _____
competing in organized sports	6. _____
practicing	7. _____
resting	8. _____
sleeping	9. _____
enjoying games	10. _____

Verbals

63 Gerunds as Subject Complements

A gerund or gerund phrase may be used as a subject complement. A subject complement completes the meaning of a linking verb.

Mom's hobby is <u>sewing</u>. (gerund)

Dad's is <u>building birdhouses</u>. (gerund phrase)

A Underline the gerund phrase in each sentence. Draw an additional line under the gerund if it is used as a subject complement. Write **DO** over any word that is the direct object of a gerund.

EXAMPLE: **My job at home is <u>washing the dishes</u>.** ^{DO}

1. Reading the newspaper is a favorite Sunday activity.

2. My usual approach is scanning the headlines.

3. Usually, poring over the sports pages takes most of Dad's time.

4. My favorite thing could never be scouring the want ads.

5. Checking the entertainment scene is something the entire family enjoys.

6. My mother's response to the editorial this week was writing her own letter.

7. Entertainment for me is laughing over the antics in my favorite comic strip.

8. Collecting characters from the *Peanuts* strip has become my brother's hobby.

9. The biggest challenge now is training my dog to bring me the newspaper.

10. Our neighbor's favorite joke is hiding the newspaper somewhere near the house.

B Complete each sentence with a phrase that contains a gerund used as the subject complement of the sentence.

1. Her favorite kind of cooking is _____ .

2. Her least favorite kind of cooking is _____ .

3. Her favorite cooking techniques are _____ .

4. Her most famous methods for cooking meat are _____ .

5. One source of relaxation for her is _____ .

6. What upset her was _____ .

7. What I don't understand is _____ .

8. Her greatest joy as a chef is _____ .

9. The most difficult part of being a chef is _____ .

10. The main job of a restaurant chef is _____ .

64 Gerunds as Direct Objects

A gerund or gerund phrase may be used as the direct object in a sentence.

Sara dislikes painting. (gerund)

Shawn enjoys reviewing movies. (gerund phrase)

A Underline the gerund phrase in each sentence. Draw an additional line under the gerund.

EXAMPLE: **The workers began laying the foundation.**

1. The master carver has started carving the limestone columns with a chisel and mallet.

2. Carvers and workers began building the Cathedral of Saint John the Divine in New York more than 100 years ago.

3. Have the quarriers finished cutting all the limestone?

4. World War II prevented their working.

5. In the 1970s the Very Reverend James Parks Morton suggested starting construction again.

6. European stonecutters undertook the training of local craftspeople.

7. The plans specify making templates for each block of stone.

8. A special arrangement involved hiring young people as apprentices.

9. Laws forbid working without protective gear.

10. People have enjoyed watching the cathedral take shape over the years.

B Use a gerund phrase from the list as a direct object to complete each sentence.

running around the track three times

selling tickets for the tournament

reading about the sport you like

comparing our scores and the pros'

going to games by car or by bus

1. The team has started _____ .

2. Do you prefer _____ ?

3. Try _____ .

4. The bowling coach enjoys _____ .

5. My workout includes _____ .

65 Gerunds as Objects of Prepositions

A gerund or gerund phrase may be used as the object of a preposition.

The group's assignment includes the task of <u>tutoring</u>. (gerund)

The time for <u>teaching the young children</u> is after school. (gerund phrase)

A Underline the gerund phrase(s) in each sentence. Draw an additional line under the gerund if it is used as the object of a preposition. Circle the preposition that introduces the gerund phrase.

EXAMPLE: Who is responsible (for) <u>calling team members</u>?

1. Being kind is one way of helping others.

2. The sentiment of caring deeply affects how a person responds to others.

3. Nothing great was ever accomplished without working hard.

4. Working for peace helps us improve our world.

5. I'm angry with Al for buying violent toys.

6. Conflict resolution is a way of solving differences peacefully.

7. Her plan for negotiating a peace treaty was approved.

8. Talking exhausted her.

9. We are indebted to the group for supporting her efforts.

10. She impressed the president by describing the difficult situation in a simple way.

B Use a phrase from the list to complete each sentence. The gerund will be the object of a preposition. Add words to fill out the sentence if you wish.

through writing   in answering   for singing

from eating   by studying

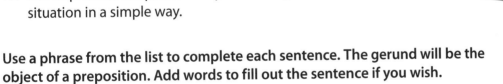

1. He was fast _____ .

2. She was known _____ .

3. You can learn _____ .

4. We can improve _____ .

5. He was sick _____ .

66 Gerunds as Appositives

A gerund or gerund phrase may be used as an appositive. An appositive is a word or group of words that follows a noun or a pronoun and helps identify it or adds information about it.

Justin's main interest, <u>acting</u>, takes most of his spare time. (gerund)

His role, <u>playing the part of an astronaut</u>, excited him. (gerund phrase)

A **Underline the gerund phrase in each sentence. Draw an additional line under the gerund if it is used as an appositive.**

1. The work of Lister, introducing antiseptics into surgery, was a medical breakthrough.

2. Laying the Atlantic cable brought fame to Cyrus Field.

3. Bell's accomplishment, transmitting the human voice over the telephone, took years of work.

4. Leo Hirshfield's legacy, developing a sweet treat named after his daughter Tootsie, is what I remember.

5. Creating labor-saving devices is the inventor's aim.

6. Garrett A. Morgan proposed using a signal to direct traffic at intersections.

7. Mass-producing goods and using interchangeable parts helped establish the automobile industry.

8. Strauss and Davis's idea, sewing pants with rivets on the seams, did work out.

9. The class assignment, writing a report on a favorite inventor, is due tomorrow.

10. Our teacher accomplished her goal, finishing the chapter.

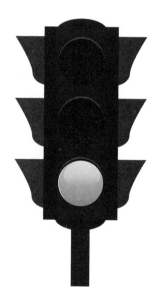

B **Complete each sentence with one of the following gerund phrases.**

cleaning out the attic   **spending time with children**

writing e-mails to friends   **becoming an astronaut**   **reading science-fiction novels**

1. Juan's task, _____ , was not easy.

2. That is Grandmother's latest accomplishment, _____ .

3. Melanie's experience, _____ , helped her get a job.

4. Donald's dream, _____ , motivated him to study hard.

5. Cindy has a favorite pastime, _____ .

Verbals

67 Possessives with Gerunds, Using *-ing* Verb Forms

Gerunds may be preceded by a possessive noun or a possessive adjective. These possessives describe the doer of the action of the gerund.

> **My deciding to go on the camping trip surprised my family.**

A verb with an *-ing* ending may be a gerund (a noun), a participle (an adjective), or a part of a verb phrase in the progressive tense.

> **Exciting adults as well as children was the aim of the trapeze artist.** (gerund)
>
> **Meanwhile, exciting the audience in the arena, acrobats performed their acts.** (participial adjective before a noun)
>
> **Their performances, exciting and courageous, left us in awe.** (participial adjective after a noun)
>
> **Every act was exciting.** (participial adjective after a linking verb)
>
> **Large elephants were exciting children in a nearby tent.** (part of a progressive verb)

A Underline the correct form.

1. (Our   Us) choosing a camping trip proved to be a good idea.
2. My brother agreed to (my   me) taking his sleeping bag.
3. The scout leader was surprised at (me   my) volunteering to put up the tent.
4. He watched (my   me), wearing a pleased expression, as I did the job efficiently.
5. (Him   His) praising me for my work made me feel good.
6. (Joe   Joe's) cooking the supper was a surprise to us.
7. (Him   His) making pioneer stew was a good idea—we loved the meal.
8. The (animals   animals') chattering far into the night kept us awake.
9. On the second night we again heard (them   their), noting that they had moved closer to our camp.
10. (Them   Their) enjoying the outdoor experience so wholeheartedly meant that the scouts would make a similar trip soon.

B Identify each italicized word ending in *-ing* as a gerund, a participial adjective, or part of a progressive verb.

_____ 1. *Singing* around the campfire was a fun part of the trip.
_____ 2. Our *singing* voices filled the night air.
_____ 3. *Singing* the entire campfire song, James proved to us that he knew all the verses.
_____ 4. We were *singing* old songs into the night.
_____ 5. After the *singing* ended, we returned to our tents.
_____ 6. *Hiking* in the woods, we learned to identify certain trees and wildlife.
_____ 7. I was *hiking* in the woods when I saw a dappled fawn.
_____ 8. *Hiking* in the woods was the highlight of the trip for me.
_____ 9. It is a good thing I had brought good *hiking* boots.
_____ 10. This *hiking* experience made me appreciate the outdoors.

68 Reviewing Gerunds

A Underline the gerund(s) in each sentence. On the line write **S** if it is the subject, **DO** if it is the direct object, **OP** if it is the object of a preposition, **SC** if it is the subject complement, and **APP** if it is an appositive.

_____ 1. The task of saving wildlife is crucial after an oil spill.

_____ 2. Cleaning the oil from sea birds is no small job.

_____ 3. In 1989 the mission of the _Exxon Valdez,_ hauling oil off the coast of Alaska, led to disaster.

_____ 4. The spilling of 11 million gallons of crude oil occurred when the tanker hit a reef.

_____ 5. One of the first tasks was locating oil-containment equipment.

_____ 6. Snow did not permit rescuers' getting the equipment quickly.

_____ 7. The job of containing the oil spill was hampered by good weather.

_____ 8. Calm winds did not permit using materials to break up the oil.

_____ 9. Using buckets to scoop up oil produced little result.

_____ 10. Crews worked at containment, keeping the oil from spreading, but their efforts weren't effective.

_____ 11. Their greatest fear, removing dead sea animals, became a reality.

_____ 12. Seeing thousands of dead birds on the beaches was heartbreaking.

_____ 13. Rescue workers took the dying animals to centers for cleaning.

_____ 14. A serious consequence of the spill, freezing because their oil-soaked fur could not provide insulation from the cold, caused the death of many otters.

_____ 15. Our job should be preventing such disasters from happening.

B Follow the instructions and write sentences using the following gerund phrase: _swimming in the lake_.

16. (Use as a subject.)_____

17. (Use as a direct object.)_____

18. (Use as a subject complement.)_____

19. (Use as the object of a preposition.)_____

20. (Use as an appositive.)_____

Verbals

69 Infinitives as Subjects

An **infinitive** is a verb form, usually preceded by *to,* that can be used as a verb, a noun, an adjective, or an adverb. An **infinitive phrase** consists of the infinitive and a direct object, a complement, or modifiers. The direct object receives the action of the infinitive. An infinitive or an infinitive phrase can be used as the subject of a sentence.

> **To hear can be difficult in a noisy room.** (infinitive)
>
> **To address an audience directly should be a speaker's main goal.**
> (infinitive phrase with direct object)

A Underline the infinitive or the infinitive phrase in each sentence. Draw an additional line under each infinitive. Write **DO** over any word that is the direct object of an infinitive.

  DO   DO
EXAMPLE: **To save lives and property is the work of a firefighter.**

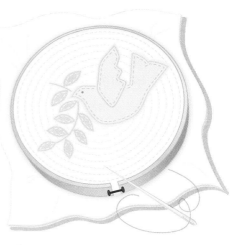

1. To solve the puzzle takes some time.

2. To hear the watchdog's bark is often frightening.

3. To have been chosen was a great honor.

4. To learn embroidery requires patient effort.

5. To drive carelessly endangers the lives of others.

6. To serve is the job of any person in the armed forces.

7. To persevere to the end demands constant effort.

8. To rescue the lost fishermen required a life raft and two sailors.

9. To join the club was the best thing Steve did.

10. To exercise daily is an excellent habit.

B Use an infinitive phrase from the list to complete each sentence.
The infinitive phrase will be the subject of the sentence.

To save money for college	To build a model ship	To travel widely
To do well in school	To hear the dog bark	

1. _____ requires great skill.

2. _____ is the goal of many people.

3. _____ is very rewarding.

4. _____ can be annoying.

5. _____ is worthwhile.

Verbals

70 Infinitives as Subject Complements

An infinitive or infinitive phrase may be used as a subject complement. A subject complement completes the meaning of a linking verb.

My greatest fear is <u>to fail</u>. (infinitive)

The recommended approach is <u>to take notes during class</u>. (infinitive phrase)

A Underline each infinitive phrase. Draw an additional line under the infinitive.

1. The life's work of Marie Curie was to study radioactive substances.

2 An early goal was to learn about radioactivity in uranium ore.

3. She and her husband were to become a team.

4. The result of their work was to discover radium and polonium, highly radioactive elements.

5. Another result would be to win a Nobel Prize in physics.

6. After her husband's death Marie Curie's distinction was to earn another Nobel Prize, this time in chemistry.

7. Her work was to isolate radium and to study its properties.

8. Another accomplishment was to start the Radium Institute in Paris.

9. Curie's idea was to take x-ray machines to the battlefields.

10. Her plan was to use x-rays for locating bullets in soldier's wounds.

B Complete each sentence with a phrase that contains an infinitive used as the subject complement.

1. A scientist's main job is _____ .

2. The object of higher education has always been _____ .

3. The aim of scientific study should be _____ .

4. The results of experimentation in the lab generally is _____ .

5. One purpose of scientific data may be _____ .

Marie Curie worked in the fields of physics and chemistry, making discoveries that continue to be of great benefit to people today. Write about a way you might work to improve the lives of others.

© Loyola Press. Exercises in English **Level H**

Verbals

Name .... Date ....

71 More Infinitives as Subjects and as Subject Complements

An infinitive or an infinitive phrase can be used as the subject or the subject complement in a sentence. Infinitives can be active or passive, and they can also have perfect forms.

SIMPLE ACTIVE	**To do the laundry** is my least favorite chore.
SIMPLE PASSIVE	The clothes in this hamper are **to be washed**.
PERFECT ACTIVE	**To have finished the laundry** will be great.
PERFECT PASSIVE	It was supposed **to have been finished by now**.

A Underline the infinitive phrase in each sentence. Identify the tense by writing **S** if it is a simple tense or **P** if it is a perfect tense. Identify the voice by writing **A** if it is active or **PA** if it is passive.

TENSE   VOICE

_____ _____ 1. The flag is to be raised at noon.

_____ _____ 2. To raise the flag is the privilege of the honor guard.

_____ _____ 3. The principal's role is to lead the Pledge of Allegiance.

_____ _____ 4. The students' duty was to have been reciting it after her.

_____ _____ 5. Then the parade is to be started.

_____ _____ 6. The school song is to be played by the pep band.

_____ _____ 7. The first float was supposed to have carried the football team.

_____ _____ 8. The float was supposed to have been driven by the coach.

_____ _____ 9. To excite the crowd is the job of the cheerleaders.

_____ _____ 10. To have a lot of fun is my expectation.

_____ _____ 11. Our goal was to make dinner by six o'clock.

_____ _____ 12. The potatoes were to have been boiled earlier in the day.

_____ _____ 13. My brother's job was to fry them with onions and celery.

_____ _____ 14. The carrots for the salad were to have been shredded by my sister.

_____ _____ 15. The lettuce was to have been washed and dried by 5:30.

_____ _____ 16. My job was to marinate the chicken.

_____ _____ 17. The chicken was to have been baked with mushroom gravy.

_____ _____ 18. Unfortunately nothing was to have happened as it did.

_____ _____ 19. To have a disaster like this was unprecedented.

_____ _____ 20. The worst part was to disappoint our parents.

72 Infinitives as Direct Objects

An infinitive or infinitive phrase may be used as the direct object in a sentence.

My aunt plans <u>to move</u>. (infinitive)

She expects <u>to buy a little house in Utah</u>. (infinitive phrase)

A Underline the infinitive phrase in each sentence. Draw an additional line under the infinitive.

      EXAMPLE: My friend never wants <u>to carry a heavy backpack</u>.

1. A lobbyist is a person who tries to influence the proceedings of Congress.
2. Young people should try to think for themselves about politics.
3. Have you begun to learn the names of the new cabinet members?
4. The new president resolved to make changes immediately.
5. The president hopes to travel to Europe.
6. The vice president promised to serve the president.
7. Republicans attempted to pass tax laws quickly.
8. Democrats wanted to slow their actions.
9. We must learn to cooperate with others on important issues.
10. The work of the men and women in Congress deserves to be praised.

B Use an infinitive phrase from the list to complete each sentence. The infinitive phrase will be the direct object of each sentence.

to drive a race car   to wrestle   to write a story

to learn all the dance steps   to prepare for tomorrow

1. Jonathan would like _____ .
2. Have the children been taught _____ ?
3. Several teammates tried _____ .
4. Before we retire, we must try _____ .
5. Does she want _____ ?

Verbals

73 Infinitives as Appositives

An infinitive or infinitive phrase may be used as an appositive. An appositive follows a noun or a pronoun and helps identify it or adds information about it.

Miguel had only one objective, <u>to win</u>. (infinitive)

We achieved our goal, <u>to earn money for charity</u>. (infinitive phrase)

A **Underline the infinitive phrase in each sentence. Draw an additional line under the infinitive.**

1. John Adams fulfilled his responsibility, to serve his country loyally, by taking on many government posts.

2. One huge task, to develop Washington, D.C. into the nation's capital, was undertaken during his presidency.

3. His main obligation, to serve as president, came first.

4. A major challenge, to avoid war with France, was settled peacefully in 1800.

5. The goal of the Federalists, to organize a strong government, was supported by Alexander Hamilton.

6. The Republicans' goal, to respond to the needs of ordinary citizens, was defended by Thomas Jefferson.

7. One aim of Adams's, to move into the president's house in Washington, was accomplished.

8. The country's potential dilemma, to have a tie vote in the electoral college, became a reality in 1800.

9. The duty of the House of Representatives, to break the tie between Jefferson and Burr, took days.

10. Finally, after 36 ballots they fulfilled their responsibility, to choose a president, and elected Jefferson.

B **Complete each sentence with one of the following infinitive phrases. The sentence will have an infinitive as an appositive.**

to study politics	to elect more minorities	to vote
to run for office	to make education a priority	

1. Their hope, _____ , will require time and effort.

2. The proposal, _____ , was raised at the town hall meeting.

3. My plan, _____ , was applauded.

4. Mrs. Hughes's decision, _____ , was difficult.

5. He had one ambition, _____ .

74 Infinitives as Adjectives

An infinitive or an infinitive phrase can be used as an adjective to describe a noun or a pronoun.

Robert Fulton is an interesting person <u>to read about</u>.

In the example above, the infinitive phrase *to read about* describes *person*.

Underline the infinitive phrase used as an adjective in each sentence. Circle the noun it describes.

1. Steam has the power to run machinery.

2. Practical ways to use steam as a source of power for machinery were developed in the 1700s.

3. Robert Fulton's *Clermont* was one of the first boats to run on steam.

4. Even as a child in Pennsylvania, he thought of many things to make.

5. One invention to be built by Fulton was a paddlewheel, which he constructed when he was 13 years old.

6. Before starting on his steamboat invention, he took time to try his hand at painting.

7. His articles to highlight the benefits of canal transportation were sent to senior U.S. officials.

8. He invented a machine to dig canal channels.

9. He designed a device to cut marble.

10. He labored on an invention to travel underwater.

11. The vehicle to be developed was actually an early submarine, but it wasn't very successful!

12. He was working at the time on weapons to be used in sea warfare.

13. His effort to build a steamboat continued after he returned to the United States.

14. The incentive to make a steamboat came from several sources.

15. A steamboat to navigate the Hudson River was his plan.

16. The race to build steamboats for transport and travel had begun.

17. Other efforts to run a steamboat occurred before and after Fulton's.

18. However, the person to be remembered as the inventor of the steamboat was Fulton.

19. Fulton had not forgotten his plan to build a submarine.

20. He did not, however, have a chance to finish it before his death in 1815.

75 Infinitives as Adverbs

An infinitive or infinitive phrase can be used as an adverb to describe a verb, an adjective, or another adverb. An infinitive that describes a verb often tells *why* or *how*.

We went to the exhibit to find out about future inventions. (describes the verb *went*)

We were happy to see so many creative ideas. (describes the adjective *happy*)

The inventors were creative enough to have many surprising inventions. (describes the adverb *enough*)

Underline the infinitive phrase used as an adverb in each sentence. Circle the word(s) it describes. Identify the word(s) as a noun, an adjective, or an adverb.

_____ 1. Our class went to the museum to see student fantasy inventions.

_____ 2. We were eager to see the students' ideas.

_____ 3. To illustrate their inventions, students drew pictures or made models of them.

_____ 4. They stood near the exhibits to answer questions from visitors.

_____ 5. One invention, a comfy chair, was designed to help people with disabilities.

_____ 6. To operate it, you pressed a button; it became a rocking chair or a chair with wheels.

_____ 7. The usefulness of that invention was easy to see.

_____ 8. To stop unwanted noise, some students had the idea of a special hat.

_____ 9. To use it, you just put it on your head, and then all traffic noise, music, or even people's voices were filtered out.

_____ 10. Many students used their creativity to help solve environmental problems.

_____ 11. One idea, a small bin, would be installed in apartment buildings to get rid of garbage.

_____ 12. The bin would separate items into various piles—glass, paper, and so on—to be recycled.

_____ 13. It also would serve to compact the garbage into tiny disposable packages.

_____ 14. To gain more living space, some students suggested a city on stilts over the ocean.

_____ 15. People would use solar panels to supply energy for such a city.

_____ 16. To clean the air, a huge de-smogger was proposed by some students.

_____ 17. The plant, with huge stacks, worked to remove pollution from the air.

_____ 18. We were in the exhibit long enough to see most of the inventions.

_____ 19. The exhibit was too big to see them all, however.

_____ 20. On exiting, we voted to choose the best invention that we'd seen.

76 Hidden Infinitives and Split Infinitives

A **hidden infinitive,** one in which the word *to* is not used, appears after certain verbs, such as *hear, see, know, feel, let, make,* and *help,* and with the prepositions *but* and *except* and the conjunction *than.*

I heard the bird <u>sing</u>.

Her stories always make me <u>cry</u>.

She does nothing but <u>study</u> all day.

I can think of many things I'd rather do than <u>clean</u> my room.

A **split infinitive** results when an adverb is placed between *to* and the verb. Split infinitives generally should be avoided.

SPLIT INFINITIVE	**Hal decided to patiently wait his turn.**
IMPROVED	**Hal decided to wait his turn patiently.**

A Underline the hidden infinitive in each sentence.

1. Will you let me hold the baby?
2. My mother does nothing but work all day.
3. All night I heard the rain pound on the roof.
4. "I thought I felt something move!" she whispered.
5. The patient did nothing but sleep after the surgery.
6. I have never seen him run so fast.
7. I heard the child cry.
8. The teacher helped the students study the new assignment.
9. Your performances always make me laugh.
10. Let not your hearts be troubled.

B Each sentence contains a split infinitive. Rewrite the sentence, placing the adverb in a better position.

1. The teacher asked us to completely erase the boards.

   _____

2. Be sure to correctly answer the essay question.

   _____

3. The doctor was unwilling to indefinitely postpone the surgery.

   _____

4. We like to slowly stroll along the beach.

   _____

5. Our family is planning to immediately leave on vacation.

   _____

77 Reviewing Infinitives

A Underline the infinitive in each sentence. On the line write **S** if it is the subject, **DO** if it is the direct object, **SC** if it is the subject complement, and **APP** if it is an appositive.

_____ 1. My sister has never learned to skate.

_____ 2. Your suggestion to travel by bus was a good idea.

_____ 3. We would prefer to go with you.

_____ 4. To write well requires practice.

_____ 5. The purpose of the game is to learn math facts.

_____ 6. Try to finish the work before noon.

_____ 7. The reason she is coming is to babysit.

_____ 8. Ms. Henry's motion, to adjourn the meeting, passed quickly.

_____ 9. To be happy is an important goal in my life.

_____ 10. My worst fear, to fail in school, motivates me.

B Write on the line whether the italicized infinitive is used as an adjective or an adverb.

_____ 11. Quarantine is sometimes necessary *to protect* others.

_____ 12. My cousin is coming *to visit* us.

_____ 13. Youth is the time *to sow* the seeds of character.

_____ 14. Philip lunged *to tackle* the quarterback.

_____ 15. They were afraid *to undertake* the journey.

_____ 16. Quotation marks are used *to enclose* the words of a speaker.

_____ 17. Efforts *to eliminate* the use of pesticides are gratifying.

_____ 18. How did our school raise the money *to build* the gym?

_____ 19. The power *to run* the mill comes from water.

_____ 20. Her desire *to improve* is impressive.

Verbals

Continued → 81

77 Reviewing Infinitives, *continued*

C **Underline the hidden infinitive in each sentence.**

21. Did you hear the dog bark?

22. She would rather learn to swim than skate.

23. Darlene does nothing but giggle when she is corrected.

24. All through the storm, we heard the wind howl.

25. Watch me dive into the pool.

D **Rewrite each sentence. Place the adverb in a better position.**

26. I expect you to wholeheartedly support me.

_____

27. The janitor does not expect to constantly pick up after us.

_____

28. To quickly eat your lunch may give you indigestion.

_____

29. To suddenly end our support would be disastrous for them.

_____

30. To positively respond to the questionnaire would aid the cause.

_____

E **Follow the instructions and write sentences using the following infinitive phrase: *to visit a foreign country.***

31. (Use as a subject.)_____

32. (Use as a direct object.)_____

33. (Use as a subject complement.)_____

34. (Use as an appositive.)_____

35. (Use as an adverb.) _____

© Loyola Press. Exercises in English **Level H**

Verbals

78 Reviewing Verbals

A Underline the participle in each sentence. Circle the word it modifies.

1. The audience applauded the couple skating in the competition.

2. The trophy won by the hockey team will be on display in the school hall.

3. Having eaten their lunch, the students went out onto the ice.

4. Spectators gathered to watch the skaters flying around the rink.

5. Ellen, having trained for years, prepared to perform.

6. The school trophy case contains the winners' names engraved in brass.

7. Vowing to return, our coach left his job temporarily.

8. Skaters trained in northern states are comfortable on the ice.

B Write a sentence, using each participial phrase.

standing on the corner   9. _____

_____

blown by the wind   10. _____

_____

having delivered the speech   11. _____

_____

C Underline the gerund in each sentence. On the line write **S** if it is the subject, **DO** if it is the direct object, **OP** if it is the object of a preposition, **SC** if it is the subject complement, and **APP** if it is an appositive.

_____ 12. My job, working in the retirement home, gives me great satisfaction.

_____ 13. My brother's chief service is reading books for people with visual impairments.

_____ 14. We show that we care by helping others.

_____ 15. I enjoy planning activities for senior citizens.

_____ 16. Working with older adults might be a career choice.

Verbals

Continued → 83

78 Reviewing Verbals, *continued*

D Follow the instructions and write sentences using the following infinitive phrase: *to attend college.*

17. (Use as a subject.)_____

18. (Use as a direct object.)_____

19. (Use as an appositive.)_____

E Underline the infinitive in each sentence. On the line write *S* if it is the subject, *DO* if it is the direct object, *SC* if it is the subject complement, and *APP* if it is an appositive.

_____ 20. Most students want to attend a good college.

_____ 21. My goal, to win a scholarship, may not be realistic.

_____ 22. To afford room and board is one reason for wanting a scholarship.

_____ 23. Most teachers try to prepare students for the future.

_____ 24. My biggest problem, to put my thoughts into writing, is something I must work on.

_____ 25. My hope is to achieve a high score.

Try It Yourself

On a separate sheet of paper, write five or six sentences about something you would like to do in the future. Be sure to use participles, gerunds, and infinitives correctly.

Check Your Own Work

Choose a piece of writing from your writing portfolio, a journal, a work in progress, an assignment from another class, or a letter. Revise it, applying the skills you have reviewed. This checklist will help you.

✔ Have you used participles, gerunds, and infinitives correctly?

✔ Have you avoided dangling participles?

✔ Have you avoided splitting the infinitives you used?

© Loyola Press. Exercises in English **Level H**

79 Types of Adverbs

An **adverb** is a word that describes a verb, an adjective, or another adverb. An adverb generally describes the time, place, manner, or degree of the word it modifies. It may also indicate affirmation (telling whether a statement is positive or giving consent or approval) or negation (expressing a negative condition or refusal).

TIME	The tide will recede <u>later</u>.	**AFFIRMATION**	Tides are <u>undoubtedly</u> amazing.
PLACE	The water will move <u>back</u>.	**NEGATION**	We could <u>not</u> explain the
MANNER	The water recedes <u>slowly</u>.		cause of tides.
DEGREE	The water was <u>very</u> cold.		

A Underline the adverb in each sentence.

1. Have you ever wondered about the cause of tides?

2. The water in the ocean and other bodies of water rises and falls periodically.

3. Two high tides and two low tides occur daily.

4. Go to the ocean shore, and there you can see the effect of the tides.

5. You can see clearly the movement of the water along the shoreline.

6. At the beach you may notice that the water moves up over several hours.

7. Soon it starts to move in the other direction, receding from the shore.

8. The gravitational pull of the moon is quite strong on Earth.

9. The moon's force pulls the water toward a point directly below the Moon and toward a point on the exact opposite side of Earth.

10. The result is that high tide occurs simultaneously on both sides of Earth.

B Underline the adverb in each sentence. On the line identify the adverb by writing **T** for time, **P** for place, **M** for manner, **D** for degree, **A** for affirmation, or **N** for negation.

_____ 1. People have long observed the tides.

_____ 2. Indeed, the regularity of tides was noted by ancient observers.

_____ 3. They carefully studied the tides.

_____ 4. Some ancients accurately theorized that a connection existed between the moon and the tides.

_____ 5. The actual connection could not be confirmed with the knowledge people had at that time.

_____ 6. Then Isaac Newton explained the basic laws of motion and gravity.

_____ 7. Tides were recognized as extremely complex occurrences.

_____ 8. Tides are a result of a fairly complicated interaction of several factors.

_____ 9. Tides for any location are predicted by past observations of tides there.

_____ 10. People work meticulously to produce complex tables of the tides.

Adverbs

80 Interrogative Adverbs

An **interrogative adverb** is used to ask a question. The interrogative adverbs are *how, when, where,* and *why*. They are used to ask about reason, place, time, or method.

REASON	**Why did you choose the ancient Romans as a topic?**
PLACE	**Where did you get the information you needed?**
TIME	**When is the report due?**
METHOD	**How did you organize your report?**

A Underline the interrogative adverb in each sentence. On the line identify what each adverb expresses by writing **R** for reason, **P** for place, **T** for Time, or M for method.

_____ 1. When was the Roman Empire at the height of its power?

_____ 2. Where was it located?

_____ 3. How did the Romans build the empire?

_____ 4. Why did the empire fall?

_____ 5. Why was a wolf with two human babies the symbol of Rome?

_____ 6. When was the city of Rome founded?

_____ 7. Why were the aqueducts built?

_____ 8. How did the aqueducts function to carry water?

_____ 9. Where did the ancient Romans go for entertainment?

_____ 10. When was the Colosseum built?

B Complete each sentence with an appropriate interrogative adverb. More than one answer may be correct in some sentences.

1. _____ is Mount Vesuvius—near Rome or near Naples?

2. _____ did the eruption of Mount Vesuvius occur—79 BC or AD 79?

3. _____ was the eruption unexpected?

4. _____ is the eruption considered important by historians?

5. _____ did archaeologists uncover the cities of Pompeii and Herculaneum?

6. _____ did the volcano destroy the cities?

7. _____ were the cities finally rediscovered?

8. _____ was the most recent eruption of Vesuvius?

9. _____ can you find information on volcanic eruptions?

10. _____ are some other active volcanoes located?

81 Adverbial Nouns

An **adverbial noun** is a noun that functions as an adverb. Generally it modifies a verb and expresses time, distance, measure, value, or direction.

The cake should bake for an hour.

TO EXPRESS	TIME	DISTANCE	MEASURE	VALUE	DIRECTION
USE WORDS SUCH AS	**hours**	**miles**	**pint**	**dollars**	**north**

A Underline each adverbial noun. Write on the line what it expresses—time, distance, measure, value, or direction.

_____ 1. Because of gold's great value, men have spent years searching for it.

_____ 2. It has been used a great deal for jewelry.

_____ 3. It can be hammered 0.000005 inch thick.

_____ 4. One ounce can be stretched 62 miles.

_____ 5. It will not melt until it reaches 1,947 degrees Fahrenheit.

_____ 6. The largest gold nugget ever found weighed 150 pounds.

_____ 7. It turned up accidentally some 130 years ago in Australia.

_____ 8. Fortune hunters headed west during the American gold rush.

_____ 9. Americans waited 41 years, until 1974, for the ban on private ownership of gold to be lifted.

_____ 10. The gold stored at Fort Knox would cost several billion dollars to buy.

B Complete each sentence with an adverbial noun that expresses the quality in italics.

time 1. The opera will last three _____ .

distance 2. The theater is seven _____ away.

direction 3. Tell the cab driver to turn _____ after the light.

time 4. We have only 15 _____ till the curtain rises.

measure 5. Earlier today the ticket line stretched three _____ .

value 6. The tickets cost 50 _____ apiece.

distance 7. The singers traveled many _____ to be here.

time 8. The star tenor arrived just this _____ .

measure 9. He lost 20 _____ on the exercise program.

time 10. His last performance in America was _____ ago.

Adverbs

82 Comparative and Superlative Adverbs

The **comparative** and **superlative** degrees of most adverbs that end in *-ly* are formed by adding *more* or *most* (or *less* or *least*) before the positive form of the adverb.

more sadly, most sadly   **less sadly, least sadly**

The comparative and superlative forms of adverbs that do not end in *-ly* are formed by adding *-er* or *-est*.

faster, fastest

Some adverbs, such as *well* and *much*, have irregular comparative and superlative forms.

A Complete the chart with degrees of comparison.

POSITIVE	COMPARATIVE	SUPERLATIVE
1. slowly	less slowly	least slowly
2. far	farther	farthest
3. badly	more badly	worst
4. noisily	more noisily	most noisily
5. soon	sooner	soonest
6. playfully	more playfully	most playfully
7. quickly	more quickly	most quickly
8. clearly	less clearly	least clearly
9. highly	more highly	most highly
10. well	weller	wellest

B Underline the adverb in each sentence. Write its degree of comparison on the line.

positive	1. Two people can often travel more cheaply than one.
positive	2. Maggie quickly realized this in Europe last summer.
comparative	3. Money stretches further when you can share travel accommodations.
positive	4. She spent her money mainly on hotels.
superlative	5. Deals on plane tickets can be made most easily when a person buys two or more.
positive	6. You can also travel more safely as a pair.
superlative	7. Criminals most often target people who are by themselves.
superlative	8. All tourists should travel most cautiously at night.
positive	9. Fortunately, Maggie was not the victim of a pickpocket.
positive	10. Planning a trip carefully will be advantageous in the long run.

Adverbs

83 As . . . As, So . . . As, and *Equally*

Adjectives and adverbs can both be used in comparisons with *as . . . as, so . . . as,* and *equally.*

When comparing people, places, or things, use only *as . . . as* in positive statements. Use either *as . . . as* or *so . . . as* in negative statements.

This year's family reunion was as successful as last year's reunion.

The weather was not so hot as (or as hot as) it was last year.

Equally means "as" when it describes an adjective. Never use *as* between *equally* and the word it describes.

CORRECT   **The first two family reunions were equally enjoyable.**

INCORRECT   **The first two family reunions were equally as enjoyable.**

A **Complete each sentence by writing *as, so,* or *equally* on the line.**

1. The picnic grounds were _____ *as* _____ crowded as they were last year.

2. The weather wasn't _____ *as* _____ cloudy last year as it was this year.

3. The food, however, was _____ *as* _____ wonderful this year as it was last year.

4. My dad's apple pies were _____ *as* _____ good as Aunt Jennie's.

5. Aunt Elaine's pies and Aunt Sally's pies were __*equally*__ delicious.

6. My cookies, however, weren't _____ *as* _____ good as Cousin June's.

7. Cousin Kara sang _____ *as* _____ well as Uncle James in the karaoke contest.

8. Peter didn't sing _____ *as* _____ well as Cousin Kara, in my opinion.

9. I thought Cousin Fred and Cousin Mike sang __*equally*__ well.

10. My pictures didn't come out _____ *as* _____ clearly as mom's.

B **Write a sentence, using each group of terms shown and *as . . . as, so . . . as,* or *equally.* Use the directions to determine the type of comparison—positive, negative, or equal.**

1. mystery novels, interesting, adventure stories (negative)

   Mystery novels weren't as interesting as adventure stories

2. Aunt Lila's photos, good, my mother's photos, impressive (equal)

   Aunt Lila's photos were equally good as my mother's photos which is impressive

3. swimming, exciting, biking (positive)

   Swimming is so exciting as biking

4. poetry, easy to read, short story (negative)

   Poetry wasn't so easy to read as short stories

5. algebra, challenging, geometry (positive)

   Algebra was as challenging as geometry

Adverbs

84 Adverb Phrases and Adverb Clauses

Prepositional phrases can be used as adverbs to describe verbs, adjectives, or other adverbs. These prepositional phrases are called **adverb phrases.** They tell when, where, who, and how.

A **clause** is a group of words that has a subject and a predicate. A dependent clause does not express a complete thought. A dependent clause that acts as an adverb is called an **adverb clause.** Some common subordinate conjunctions used to introduce adverb clauses are *after, although, as, because, if, since, so that, unless, until, when, whenever, wherever, whether,* and *while.*

A Underline the adverb phrase in each sentence. Circle the word(s) it describes.

1. Winston Churchill originally trained for a military career.

2. During his lifetime Churchill held numerous political offices.

3. He led Great Britain at a difficult time.

4. Churchill was prime minister during World War II.

5. Much of the European continent had been conquered by Hitler's German armies.

6. The island of Britain was besieged by enemies.

7. Through his courage and eloquence, Churchill inspired the British people.

8. Eventually the United States and the Soviet Union joined with Britain.

9. They fought against Germany and the other Axis powers.

10. The terrible war ended in 1945.

B Underline the adverb clause in each sentence. Circle the verb(s) it describes.

1. As a boy, Winston Churchill was a poor student although he was intelligent.

2. After he served as a soldier, he became a politician.

3. Churchill was serving as prime minister when Britain faced the loss of its freedom.

4. Wherever he went during the dark days of the war, he held his fingers in a *V* formation to symbolize *victory.*

5. If he hadn't shown such courage, Britain might have been defeated.

> *Winston Churchill acted with courage and compassion during a difficult time. Not everyone will lead a country, but everyone can act with courage and compassion. Tell about a time when you have acted bravely and compassionately.*

Adverbs

85 Reviewing Adverbs

A **Underline each adverb. On the line write its type—time, place, degree, manner, affirmation, negation.**

_____ 1. Christopher Columbus sailed westward from Spain in 1492.

_____ 2. He was actually looking for Asia when he landed in America.

_____ 3. Christopher Columbus is often credited with America's discovery.

_____ 4. But civilizations were already here when he arrived.

_____ 5. Many were highly developed cultures.

B **Complete each question with an appropriate interrogative adverb.**

6. _____ did the first people to reach America come from?

7. _____ did they come to America?

8. _____ did they manage to get to a continent surrounded by water?

9. _____ did they go after they got here?

10. _____ was their biggest challenge?

C **Underline the adverb in each sentence. On the line write its degree of comparison— positive, comparative, or superlative.**

_____ 11. The first Americans most likely came by way of the Bering Strait.

_____ 12. The Bering Strait is widely believed to have been solid ice.

_____ 13. Scholars generally agree that the earliest settlers were from north Asia.

_____ 14. These first Americans were most probably nomadic peoples.

_____ 15. Scarcity forced them to search farther for their food.

Adverbs

Continued →

85 Reviewing Adverbs, *continued*

D Write on the line whether each italicized word is an adjective or an adverb.

_____ 16. *Most* Native American cultures had developed agriculture by 2000 BC.

_____ 17. Maize was the *most* commonly grown grain.

_____ 18. Livestock was *less* important to Native American cultures.

_____ 19. Protein was obtained *primarily* from plants.

_____ 20. *Additional* protein was acquired through hunting and fishing.

E Underline each adverb phrase once and each adverb clause twice. A sentence may have a phrase, a clause, or both. Circle the word(s) the phrase or the clause modifies.

21. Astronauts float in space, our science teacher said, because there is no gravity.

22. Gravity is what holds people down; if there weren't any gravity, they would float everywhere.

23. Yesterday our class performed a gravity experiment in the lab.

24. Although we were careful, it did not work.

25. We should have read the lab manual before we started.

26. I repeated the experiment several times by myself.

27. Unfortunately, I failed in every attempt.

28. Even though I didn't succeed, I may try again.

29. Since there is gravity everywhere on Earth, my experiments are probably permanently doomed.

30. Eventually, as an astronaut, I'll fly to the moon and personally experience the lack of gravity.

Try It Yourself

On a separate sheet of paper, write five or six sentences about something you have learned to do recently. Be sure to use adverbs correctly.

Check Your Own Work

Choose a selection from your writing portfolio, a journal, a work in progress, an assignment from another class, or a letter. Revise it, applying the skills you have reviewed. This checklist will help you.

✔ Have you included appropriate adverbs?

✔ Have you distinguished between adjectives and adverbs?

✔ Have you used the comparison of adverbs correctly?

86 Single and Multiword Prepositions

A **preposition** shows the relationship between a noun or a pronoun and some other word in a sentence. A **prepositional phrase** is composed of the preposition, the object of the preposition, and words that describe the object. A **multiword preposition** is made up of more than one word but is treated as a single word. Common multiword prepositions are *according to, because of, in spite of, instead of,* and *on account of.*

SINGLE	Cougar is another name <u>for</u> a puma.
MULTIWORD	<u>According to</u> this article, pumas are endangered.

A Underline the preposition or prepositions in each sentence. Circle the object of each preposition.

1. Pumas are among the rarest animals in the world.

2. Pumas are found from British Columbia to Patagonia.

3. Without protection they stand little chance of survival.

4. Their coats range from a reddish-brown color to a bluish-gray hue.

5. A puma's body can measure six feet long, even without its tail.

6. A puma has a small head with black spots above the eyes.

7. The cry of a puma often sounds like a person's voice.

8. Pumas sometimes attack cattle on ranches.

9. Because of such attacks, pumas have purposely been exterminated in some areas.

10. In addition to such extermination campaigns, encroachment into their territory by humans has also reduced their numbers.

B Complete each sentence with one of the prepositions listed below. Use each preposition once.

against   as   because of   in   of

1. Leopards are large members _____ the cat family.

2. They live _____ the Eastern Hemisphere only.

3. They are known _____ fierce hunters.

4. _____ their lovely black-spotted coats, they are hunted by humans.

5. Many countries have laws _____ this fur trading.

Prepositions

87 Troublesome Prepositions

You need to be careful to use certain prepositions correctly.

Beside means "at the side of or next to"; *besides* means "in addition to."

Between is used when speaking of two people, places, or things; *among* is used in speaking of more than two.

In denotes position within; *into* denotes motion or change of position.

Differ with denotes disagreement; *differ from* denotes that two things or people are not the same.

One is *angry with* a person but *angry at* a thing.

From means "coming from the possession of someone"; *off* means "away from."

A **Circle the correct preposition in parentheses.**

1. There is a pond ((beside) besides) Eva's house.
2. Many frogs lay their eggs ((in) into) this water.
3. Tadpole is a stage (among (between)) egg and frog.
4. A tadpole will later turn (in (into)) a frog.
5. Eva gets angry (with (at)) the noisy frogs when she is in bed.
6. Eva got advice (off (from)) a pet-shop owner.
7. She ((differed with) differed from) him on how to handle a pet frog.
8. Toads differ ((from) with) frogs in that toads spend most of their lives on land.
9. (Beside (Besides)) this difference, toads have warts but frogs do not.
10. Frogs are found ((in) into) a greater variety of climates than toads are.

B **Complete each sentence with a correct preposition.**

1. A caterpillar will eventually turn __into__ a butterfly.
2. Did you study the debate __about__ Lincoln and Douglas?
3. The candy was equally distributed __to__ the triplets.
4. _____ *Stuart Little*, E. B. White also wrote *Charlotte's Web*.
5. Mr. Blair was angry __with__ his son for breaking the window.
6. Mark differs __with__ Jim often over who should clean the bird cage.
7. The coach was angry __at__ all the errors in the news report.
8. The trees differ __from__ each other in more ways than one.
9. He does not look so tall when he stands __beside__ the basketball player.
10. The broom belongs __in__ the closet when it's not being used.

88 Words Used as Adverbs and Prepositions

Some words can be used as adverbs or as prepositions. A **preposition** takes an object; the preposition with its object shows a relationship to another word in the sentence. An **adverb** tells how, when, where, why, to what extent, and under what condition. It modifies a verb, an adjective, or another adverb, and it does not have an object.

| PREPOSITION | **Jack fell down the hill.** |
| ADVERB | **Jack fell down.** |

A On the line write **A** if the italicized word is an adverb or **P** if it is a preposition.

_____ 1. The Eiffel Tower is one of the seven wonders *of* the modern world.

_____ 2. It is located *in* Paris, France.

_____ 3. The Eiffel Tower is *on* the bank of the Seine River.

_____ 4. The tower was built *by* the engineer Alexandre-Gustave Eiffel.

_____ 5. It tapers *upward* to a height of 984 feet.

_____ 6. One may walk *up* or take an elevator.

_____ 7. Every day thousands of people go to the top to look *around*.

_____ 8. From the very top a person can see clear *across* Paris.

_____ 9. If I were at the top, I would be afraid to look *down*.

_____ 10. The uppermost platform is almost 1,000 feet *from* the ground.

B Write sentences, using each word as an adverb.

away   1. _____

in   2. _____

over   3. _____

before   4. _____

around   5. _____

C Write sentences using each word as a preposition.

near   1. _____

beyond   2. _____

down   3. _____

between   4. _____

off   5. _____

89 Prepositional Phrases as Adjectives

A prepositional phrase that describes a noun or a pronoun is an **adjective phrase**.

I read a book about Anne Sullivan.

Underline the adjective phrase in each sentence. Circle the word it describes.

1. Anne Sullivan was the famous teacher of Helen Keller's.
2. Helen was a person without sight or hearing.
3. Anne herself had difficulty with her sight.
4. This problem was the result of a childhood illness.
5. Anne went to a school for blind students.
6. She graduated at the top of her class.
7. Earlier she had lived in a home for orphans.
8. Several operations on her eyes restored some of her vision.
9. Later she accepted the position as Helen's teacher.
10. Anne used a system of touch teaching.
11. Finger movements spelled the letters of the alphabet.
12. Helen did not comprehend the idea behind the movements initially.
13. Soon, however, she grasped the meaning of the movements.
14. The association between the letters and real-world objects became clear.
15. Helen's progress in her studies was amazing.
16. She eventually became a student at a prestigious college.
17. Anne accompanied her and provided help with her studies.
18. Both Anne and Helen became advocates for education rights.
19. They strongly supported education for blind people.
20. Together, they gave lectures about this need.
21. It is said that Anne's gift to Helen was words.
22. Meanwhile, Helen gave Anne a sense of family.
23. The public's interest in their story was enormous.
24. Their story became the topic of a well-known play.
25. This story remains an inspiration to all.

Anne Sullivan persevered in teaching young Helen Keller because Anne believed in what she was doing. Give an example of something you believe in strongly. How are you working to incorporate that belief into your daily life? Write about it.

© Loyola Press. Exercises in English. Level H

90 Prepositional Phrases as Adverbs

Prepositional phrases can be used as adverbs—to describe verbs, adjectives, or other adverbs. Prepositional phrases used in this way are **adverb phrases.** They answer the questions how, when, where, why, to what extent, and under what condition.

VERB	**Many people season food <u>with garlic</u>.**
ADJECTIVE	**They usually consider garlic healthful <u>for them</u>.**
ADVERB	**The waiter talks confidently <u>for someone</u> who just started work.**

A Circle the word(s) that each italicized adverb phrase describes. On the line write the part of speech for the circled word(s)—**V** for verb, **ADJ** for adjective, or **ADV** for adverb.

_____ 1. You probably have tasted garlic *in pasta sauce.*

_____ 2. It is important *in Italian and other Mediterranean cuisines.*

_____ 3. *For centuries* people have eaten garlic.

_____ 4. They also have used it *in medicines.*

_____ 5. Early *in history* people discovered garlic's healing properties.

B Underline the adverb phrase(s) in each sentence. Circle the word or word phrase it describes.

1. Garlic's strong odor protects the plant from insects and bacteria.

2. The smell comes from the chemical compound allicin.

3. In recent years scientists have studied this compound.

4. They have found that the compound is responsible for garlic's healing properties.

5. It is said to be effective against high blood pressure, diabetes, and diarrhea.

6. Allicin may also be useful in cell destruction.

7. Scientists could use the compound against cancer cells.

8. In the future allicin may combat cancer and other tumors.

9. It may even prevent weight gain and may lead to weight loss.

10. Garlic has been used as a medicine for centuries.

11. The ancient Chinese put garlic into a solution.

12. According to folk tradition,the resulting mixture cured dysentery.

13. From Egyptian hieroglyphics we know that workers who built the pyramids were given garlic.

14. It was provided for its strength-producing effects.

15. During World War I it was used to prevent gangrene if other drugs ran out.

91 Prepositional Phrases as Nouns

A prepositional phrase can be used as a noun. It can be used as a subject or a subject complement.

Before bed is not a good time to eat.

A Underline the prepositional phrase used as a noun in each sentence. On the line write **S** if it is used as the subject or **SC** if it is used as the subject complement.

_____ 1. After meals is an ideal time to brush your teeth.

_____ 2. Another good time is before bed.

_____ 3. In the morning is an important time to eat something for needed energy.

_____ 4. After school is when you might have a snack, like a piece of fruit.

_____ 5. Without butter is the way many people prefer to eat their baked potatoes.

_____ 6. My mother's coffee preference is with sugar and cream.

_____ 7. On the U.S. Department of Agriculture Web site is a good place to find the food pyramid.

_____ 8. One possible place to exercise is in a gym.

_____ 9. In the park, however, seems to be the favorite exercise area for athletes in my neighborhood.

_____ 10. On foot is a healthful way to get from place to place and from one floor to another.

B Complete each sentence with a prepositional phrase used as a subject.

1. _____ is a good place to study.

2. _____ seems to be the right time to study.

3. _____ is a good way to study.

4. _____ can be an effective way to research information.

5. _____ was where the car skidded.

C Complete each sentence with a prepositional phrase used as a subject complement.

1. My favorite spot for swimming was _____ .

2. The place to attach the label is _____ .

3. The best debates are _____ .

4. Our dog's hiding places were _____ .

5. My dad's next business trip may be _____ .

92 Reviewing Prepositions

A Underline the preposition(s) in each sentence. Circle the object of each.

1. The sperm whale has the heaviest brain of any animal.
2. The brain of this type of whale can exceed 20 pounds.
3. The human brain has a weight of less than three pounds.
4. A sperm whale's teeth can be eight inches in length.
5. This whale has teeth only on its lower jaw.

B Circle the correct preposition in parentheses.

6. There are many differences (among between) whales and fish.
7. Most important, whales differ (from with) fish in that whales are mammals.
8. (Beside Besides) this difference, whales move their tail fins up and down, not back and forth.
9. Whales are found (in into) all the world's oceans and even a few rivers.
10. Most whales gather (in into) groups when they migrate.

C On the line write **A** if the italicized word is an adverb or **P** if it is a preposition.

_____ 11. Many scientists now believe that the ancestors of whales lived *on* land.

_____ 12. These creatures foraged for food *along* the ocean shore.

_____ 13. Eighty million years passed *by*.

_____ 14. The animals gradually evolved *into* whales.

_____ 15. They went through an amphibious, seal-like stage as time went *on*.

D On the line write **ADJ** if the italicized prepositional phrase is used as an adjective, **ADV** if used as an adverb, or **N** if used as a noun.

_____ 16. Sperm whales live *in social groups.*

_____ 17. Groups *of females, calves, and young males* live together.

_____ 18. *Near the poles* is the summer home of older males.

_____ 19. *At six or seven,* the young males leave the group.

_____ 20. They join *with the older males.*

_____ 21. Sperm whales can dive *to great depths.*

_____ 22. Sperm whales live on a diet *of squid.*

_____ 23. They may be able to capture squid more easily far *under the water.*

_____ 24. The movements of the squid may be more lethargic *because of less available oxygen.*

_____ 25. The teeth on the lower jaw of a sperm whale fit into empty sockets *in the upper jaw.*

Continued →

92 Reviewing Prepositions, *continued*

E Underline the prepositional phrase(s) in each sentence. Above each phrase write *ADJ* if it is used as an adjective, *ADV* if used as an adverb, or *N* if used as a noun.

26. A broad term for whales is cetacean.

27. This comes from the Latin word for whale.

28. Whales can be divided into two groups.

29. Toothed whales have teeth, and baleen whales have no teeth but have jaws with plates.

30. These baleen plates resemble the material in human fingernails.

31. A baleen whale swims with a wide-open mouth and gathers plankton, filtering it through the plates.

32. Under the water is the place where whales feed.

33. A whale can hold its breath a long time because of a special chemical.

34. This chemical, called myoglobin, carries oxygen throughout the body.

35. Whales have larger amounts of this chemical than land mammals do.

Try It Yourself

On a separate sheet of paper, write about something that you have recently studied in school or something that you have recently learned that interests you. Use prepositions in your sentences.

Check Your Own Work

Choose a selection from your writing portfolio, a journal, a work in progress, an assignment from another class, or a letter. Revise it, applying the skills you have reviewed. This checklist will help you.

✔ Have you used prepositional phrases to add details to your sentences?

✔ Have you used troublesome prepositions correctly, such as *beside, besides; in, into; between, among; differ with,* and *differ from*?

93 Sentences

A **sentence** is a group of words that expresses a complete thought. The essential parts of a sentence are a subject and a predicate. The **subject** names the person, place, or thing the sentence is about. The **predicate** tells what the subject is or does. Every sentence begins with a capital letter.

COMPLETE SUBJECT	COMPLETE PREDICATE
The solar system	contains eight major planets.
All the planets in the solar system	orbit the sun.

A Write **S** on the line if the words form a sentence and leave the line blank if they do not. Put a period at the end of each sentence.

_____ 1. All the planets move in elliptical orbits

_____ 2. The orbits of Earth and Venus are almost circular

_____ 3. Mercury and Pluto

_____ 4. Jupiter's diameter is 11 times larger than Earth's diameter

_____ 5. Only a tenth the diameter of the sun

B Read each sentence. Draw a line between the subject and the predicate.

1. Neptune is the eighth planet from the sun.

2. A hollowed-out Neptune could hold nearly 60 Earths.

3. One orbit of the Sun takes Neptune 165 years.

4. A day on Neptune is about 16 hours long.

5. The spaceship *Voyager* discovered six of Neptune's eight moons.

6. Methane gas gives Neptune its blue color.

7. Several large dark spots can be seen on the surface of Neptune.

8. The largest of these spots is about the size of Earth.

9. *Voyager* revealed long, bright clouds high in Neptune's atmosphere.

10. These clouds cast shadows on the cloud decks below.

11. The strongest winds on any planet are those on Neptune.

12. Wind speeds on Neptune reach nearly 1,200 miles per hour.

13. Neptune has a narrow, faint set of rings.

14. The four rings of Neptune are made of dust particles.

15. Scientists all over the world are studying this fascinating planet.

94 Declarative Sentences and Interrogative Sentences

A **declarative sentence** makes a statement. A declarative sentence ends with a period.

Levi Strauss was born in Bavaria in 1829.

An **interrogative sentence** asks a question. An interrogative sentence ends with a question mark.

What is Levi Strauss famous for?

Decide whether each sentence is declarative or interrogative. Write your answer on the line. Add the correct end punctuation.

_____ 1. Levi Strauss moved to San Francisco in 1850

_____ 2. What was his reason for moving

_____ 3. He wanted to strike it rich during the gold rush

_____ 4. Did he look for gold

_____ 5. Strauss had trained to be a tailor

_____ 6. He planned to manufacture tents for the miners

_____ 7. Business was not as good as he had hoped

_____ 8. What did he decide to do then

_____ 9. Strauss had brought heavy canvas to use in making tents

_____ 10. He decided to use the canvas to make pants for the miners

_____ 11. The pants were very sturdy

_____ 12. The miners found the pants perfect for their work

_____ 13. Strauss opened a factory in San Francisco

_____ 14. Did he change the pants in any way

_____ 15. He added rivets at stress points in the pants

_____ 16. A heavy blue denim material was substituted for the canvas

_____ 17. Levi Strauss's company is still in business

_____ 18. The pants he made are still called Levi's

_____ 19. Levi Strauss died in San Francisco in 1902

_____ 20. Have you ever worn a pair of Levi's

95 Imperative and Exclamatory Sentences

An **imperative sentence** gives a command or makes a request. An imperative sentence ends with a period. The subject *you* is understood.

> **Investigate the law of gravity.**

An **exclamatory sentence** expresses a strong emotion. An exclamatory sentence ends with an exclamation point.

> **That's incredible!**

A **Underline the sentences that are imperatives.**

1. Get some modeling clay, a marble or a ball bearing, a ruler, and a cookie sheet.

2. Mold the modeling clay into a flat rectangle.

3. Place the clay on a cookie sheet.

4. Drop the marble or ball bearing into the clay.

5. The object will make a dent in the clay.

6. Drop the object from various heights.

7. Measure the size of the dent each time.

8. Record your results.

9. What happens as you drop the object from greater heights?

10. Objects that fall farther are traveling faster when they hit the ground.

B **Decide whether each sentence is imperative or exclamatory. Write your answer on the line. Add the correct end punctuation.**

_____ 1. Use a heavy ball bearing, a marble, and a cookie sheet

_____ 2. Put the cookie sheet on the floor

_____ 3. Stand up very straight

_____ 4. Oh, how tilted you are

_____ 5. Be sure you keep your balance

_____ 6. Hold the ball bearing in one hand and the marble in the other

_____ 7. Raise your hands over your head

_____ 8. Drop the two objects at the same time

_____ 9. Listen for when they hit the cookie sheet

_____ 10. Yikes, they missed the cookie sheet

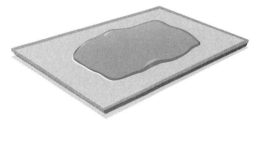

Sentences

96 The Four Kinds of Sentences

A sentence can be declarative, interrogative, imperative, or exclamatory.

Decide if each sentence is declarative, interrogative, imperative, or exclamatory. Write your answer on the line. Add the correct end punctuation.

_____ 1. Frederick Douglass was born into slavery in 1818

_____ 2. As a small child, Douglass lived with his grandmother

_____ 3. Why didn't he live with his mother

_____ 4. His mother had to work long hours in the corn fields

_____ 5. Goodness, that's a sad situation

_____ 6. When he was eight years old, Douglass was sent to live in Baltimore

_____ 7. His owner's wife, Sophia Auld, taught him the alphabet

_____ 8. Sophia's husband made her stop

_____ 9. It was illegal to teach slaves to read

_____ 10. How did Douglass finally learn to read and write

_____ 11. He had some neighborhood boys teach him

_____ 12. As a teenager, Douglass had to work as a field hand

_____ 13. He was whipped unmercifully

_____ 14. Oh my, his life was terrible

_____ 15. At the age of 20, Douglass dressed up as a sailor and escaped

_____ 16. What a brave young man he was

_____ 17. Douglass became a lecturer and a newspaper publisher

_____ 18. He worked for justice and opportunity for black people and for women

_____ 19. Where can you learn more about Frederick Douglass

_____ 20. Find out about his meetings with Abraham Lincoln

Frederick Douglass used the power of language to create positive change. Give an example of how you can use language to change things for the better.

97 Simple Subjects and Simple Predicates

The essential parts of a sentence are the subject and the predicate. The **simple subject** is the noun or pronoun that names the person, place, or thing the sentence is about. The **simple predicate** is the verb that tells what the subject does or is.

SIMPLE SUBJECT	SIMPLE PREDICATE
People	**celebrate.**
Native people	**celebrated** social occasions.
Native people of the Northwest coast	**celebrated** social occasions with potlatches.

A Write each simple subject and simple predicate in the correct column.

SIMPLE SUBJECT	SIMPLE PREDICATE
_____	_____
_____	_____
_____	_____
_____	_____
_____	_____
_____	_____
_____	_____
_____	_____
_____	_____
_____	_____

1. A potlatch often marked an event in a family's life.

2. The family celebrated a birth, a marriage, or a death.

3. The host family made elaborate preparations.

4. The lavish preparations included huge amounts of food.

5. Dishes at a potlatch often contained fish or seal meat.

6. High-ranking individuals ate the choicest dishes.

7. Diners dipped their food in seal oil.

8. Guests at the potlatch received extravagant gifts.

9. Potlatches also featured speeches, singing, and dancing.

10. Every event highlighted the host's wealth and status.

B Draw one line under the simple subject of each sentence. Draw two lines under the simple predicate.

1. Parties are still important events for native peoples of the Northwest coast.

2. A family often spends a whole year planning for a family celebration.

3. Hundreds of people gather together over a weekend.

4. The host family provides food, snacks, beverages, and entertainment.

5. Honored guests receive cash and other gifts.

98 Complete Subjects and Complete Predicates

The **complete subject** is the simple subject with all the words and phrases that describe it.
The **complete predicate** is the simple predicate with all the words and phrases that describe it.

COMPLETE SUBJECT	COMPLETE PREDICATE
The city of Johnstown, Pennsylvania,	**had a population of about 30,000.**

SIMPLE SUBJECT	SIMPLE PREDICATE
city	**had**

Draw a vertical line between the complete subject and the complete predicate of each sentence. Draw one line under the simple subject. Draw two lines under the simple predicate.

1. Johnstown was a growing and industrious community.

2. The town lay on a flood plain between two rivers.

3. The growing community narrowed the riverbanks to gain building space.

4. The South Fork Dam protected the citizens of Johnstown.

5. The dam was situated 450 feet above the town.

6. It prevented the waters of Lake Conemaugh from flooding the city.

7. The people in town worried about the dam.

8. Engineers found the dam weak and unsafe.

9. Heavy rains began to fall on May 30, 1889.

10. The dam could not withstand the pressure.

11. The dam burst at 4:07 p.m. on May 31.

12. Inhabitants of the city heard a roar like thunder.

13. Twenty million tons of water rushed through Johnstown.

14. The wall of floodwater rose to a height of 60 feet.

15. The huge wave crashed down the valley at 40 miles per hour.

16. The flood destroyed most of the major buildings in the city.

17. The raging water carried everything with it—trees, animals, and people.

18. More than 2,200 people died.

19. Thousands of other people suffered injuries.

20. The Johnstown Flood was the worst flood in U.S. history.

99 Compound Subjects and Compound Predicates

A **compound subject** consists of more than one simple subject.

> <u>People</u> and <u>animals</u> eat plants.

A **compound predicate** consists of more than one simple predicate.

> Food from plants <u>satisfies</u> hunger and <u>provides</u> nutrients.

A Each sentence has a compound subject or a compound predicate. Draw a vertical line between the subject and the predicate. Underline the compound subject or the compound predicate.

1. People and animals have lived together for thousands of years.

2. The earliest peoples hunted and killed animals for food.

3. Eventually they domesticated some animals and began to raise them.

4. Cattle, sheep, and goats provided people with meat and milk.

5. Sheep and goats also provided wool for clothing.

B Underline the simple subject(s) in each sentence. Circle the simple predicate(s).

1. Today many people own and care for pets.

2. More than 65 million pet dogs and about 75 million pet cats live in the United States.

3. Some dogs and cats care for their owners.

4. Service animals and therapy animals assist people with disabilities.

5. Guide dogs navigate for sightless people and lead them around obstacles.

6. Signal dogs listen for sounds and alert their deaf owners.

7. Both cats and dogs act as therapy animals.

8. Therapy animals visit hospitals and interact with the patients.

9. The patients pet the animals and play with them.

10. The animals amuse the patients and make them feel better.

100 Direct Objects

A **direct object** is the noun or the pronoun that answers the question *whom* or *what* after an action verb. Many sentences need direct objects to complete their meaning. A direct object may be compound.

SUBJECT	VERB	DIRECT OBJECT
The children	are studying	Navajo <u>arts</u> and <u>culture</u>.
They	found	<u>information</u> on the Internet.

A Circle the direct object(s) in each sentence.

1. The earliest Navajo used deerskins to make clothing.
2. Later the men wore cotton or velvet shirts, breeches, and moccasins.
3. Women wore dresses made of plain, dark cloth.
4. The Navajo built round houses of logs, brush, and earth.
5. Each of these hogans represented the religion or philosophy of its owner.
6. They welcomed the morning sun.
7. Navajo artists created beautiful blankets and jewelry.
8. Sand painting played a major role in ceremonies.
9. Most sand paintings required many hours and much skill to create.
10. Some ceremonies included eight or nine different sand paintings.

B Complete each sentence by writing one or more direct objects.

1. Every day I use _____ .
2. At school I often write _____ .
3. At home I often play _____ .
4. For dessert I can make _____ .
5. On the weekends I sometimes buy _____ .

© Loyola Press. Exercises in English **Level H**

Sentences

101 Indirect Objects

Some sentences have two objects—a direct object and an indirect object. The **indirect object** is the noun or pronoun that tells *to whom, for whom, to what,* or *for what* the action is done. An indirect object may be compound. In order for a sentence to have an indirect object, it must have a direct object.

> **The artist sold Alice the picture.**
>
> **Alice bought her mother and father the picture.**

A Circle the indirect object(s) in each sentence. The direct object is in italics.

1. The principal promised the students a spring *party*.

2. The children sent their parents and friends *invitations*.

3. The teachers showed the students the *schedule* of athletic events.

4. The coach told the athletes the *rules*.

5. He assigned certain players key *positions*.

6. The music teacher taught the orchestra and the chorus a new *song*.

7. She gave each member a *copy* of the music.

8. The merchant sold the girls and boys *supplies* to make posters.

9. He also offered them his *help*.

10. The committee wrote everyone a thank-you *note*.

B Underline the direct object in each sentence. Circle the indirect object(s).

1. The reporter asked the factory owner a question about pollution.

2. The owner didn't give the reporter a very clear answer.

3. The reporter showed the men and women in the audience a court order.

4. The order denied observers access to the property.

5. The factory owner promised everyone a complete explanation.

102 Adjective Phrases and Adverb Phrases

A **phrase** is a group of words that is used as a single part of speech. Unlike a sentence or clause, a phrase does not have a subject or a predicate. A phrase can be one of several types.

PARTICIPIAL	The inventor, <u>thinking creatively</u>, solved the problem.
INFINITIVE	<u>To win</u>, Ellen needed a solution.
GERUND	The whole class enjoys <u>solving problems</u>.
PREPOSITIONAL	Ms. Guerra divided the class <u>into teams</u>.

A prepositional phrase consists of a preposition and its object, which is a noun or a pronoun. A prepositional phrase can be used as an adjective or an adverb.

ADJECTIVE PHRASE	The original plan <u>for the game</u> was too complicated.
ADVERB PHRASE	<u>On Monday</u> we found the answer.

On the first line, identify each italicized phrase according to type. If it is a prepositional phrase, on the second line write how it is used— **ADJ** for adjective or **ADV** for adverb. Otherwise leave the second line blank.

_____ _____ 1. Basketball was invented *in 1891*.

_____ _____ 2. At that time no major sport was played *during the winter months*.

_____ _____ 3. James A. Naismith's ambition was *to provide an interesting sport*.

_____ _____ 4. Naismith, *having little money*, nailed up peach baskets.

_____ _____ 5. Another piece of equipment *for the new game* was a tall ladder.

_____ _____ 6. The players were divided *into two teams*.

_____ _____ 7. *Using an old soccer ball*, the teams began to play.

_____ _____ 8. *To score*, a player would throw the ball into the opposite team's basket.

_____ _____ 9. There was not a standard number of players *on a team*.

_____ _____ 10. *Watching the first game* led Naismith to draft the original 13 rules of play.

_____ _____ 11. Changes *to the game* were soon adopted.

_____ _____ 12. Metal hoops *with net bags* replaced the baskets.

_____ _____ 13. *Pulling a cord on the net* released the ball.

_____ _____ 14. Baskets with bottomless nets came into use *about 1913*.

_____ _____ 15. The game of basketball has spread *throughout the world*.

James Naismith used little money but a lot of imagination to develop a new sport. How can you use your imagination to teach or entertain people?

103 Adjective Clauses

A **clause** is a group of words that contains a subject and a predicate. An **independent clause** expresses a complete thought and can stand on its own as a sentence. A **dependent clause** does not express a complete thought and cannot stand alone as a sentence.

DEPENDENT   **INDEPENDENT**

Although only the pyramids still stand, the list of wonders has survived.

An **adjective clause,** one type of dependent clause, modifies a noun or a pronoun. An adjective clause usually begins with a **relative pronoun** (who, whom, whose, which, that) or a **subordinate conjunction** (when, where, why).

The wonder that I would most like to have seen was the Colossus of Rhodes.

A Write on the line whether each clause is independent or dependent.

_____   1. the Pharos of Alexandria was an ancient lighthouse

_____   2. because the bonfire burned continuously

_____   3. the bonfire served as a beacon

_____   4. when sailors saw the light

_____   5. as the ships approached the rocks

B Underline the adjective clause in each sentence. Circle the word(s) it modifies.

1. People travel to Egypt to see the pyramids that were built more than 4,000 years ago.

2. The pyramids are the only ancient wonder that is still in existence.

3. The Great Pyramid was built as a tomb for Khufu, who was known to the Greeks as Cheops.

4. The pyramids, which are made of millions of stone blocks, are an engineering marvel.

5. Archaeologists who have studied the pyramids think as many as 100,000 men worked 20 years or more to build the Great Pyramid.

6. The blocks of stone that were hauled into place each weighed about 2.5 tons.

7. The Great Pyramid, which rose to a finished height of about 480 feet, was built in layers of stone blocks.

8. Each layer, which fit atop the previous one, covered a smaller area.

9. The stones were dragged up a ramp, which was made higher for each layer.

10. The finished structure, which looked like a set of stairs, was then filled in with white limestone.

104 More Adjective Clauses

Remember that an **adjective clause** is a dependent clause used as an adjective. It modifies a noun or a pronoun and is usually introduced by a relative pronoun.

A **Rewrite each sentence, adding an adjective clause to modify the italicized word.**

1. My *neighbor* has a pizza business.

   _____

2. The *business* intrigued me.

   _____

3. Each weekend I talked to *Mr. Hawkins* about the business.

   _____

4. He offered me a part-time *position*.

   _____

5. Every weekend I worked the late *shift*.

   _____

6. During that time, I learned all the aspects of *pizza making*.

   _____

7. *Working* with the customers was quite a challenge.

   _____

8. My *boss* taught me that the customer is always right.

   _____

9. His *patience* is amazing.

   _____

10. Now we are working toward opening a pizza parlor at a second *location*.

    _____

    _____

B **Write sentences, using an adjective clause to modify each noun.**

homework	1. _____
television	2. _____
amusement park	3. _____
gift	4. _____
holiday	5. _____

105 Restrictive and Nonrestrictive Clauses

Some adjective clauses are essential to the meaning of sentences. These essential clauses are called **restrictive clauses.** An adjective clause that is not essential and that can be removed without changing the meaning of the sentence is called a **nonrestrictive clause.** Nonrestrictive clauses are set off by commas.

RESTRICTIVE	We read about a saint <u>who was a martyr.</u>
NONRESTRICTIVE	The martyr, <u>who sacrificed his life at an early age,</u> died for his faith.

A Underline the adjective clause in each sentence. On the line write *R* if it is restrictive or *N* if it is nonrestrictive.

_____ 1. Maximilian Kolbe, who was a martyred Catholic priest, is considered a hero.

_____ 2. He had founded a religious group whose aim was to fight evil by living a good life and praying.

_____ 3. In 1939 the Germans invaded Poland, which was Kolbe's home.

_____ 4. He and other friars helped people who were being persecuted by the Nazis.

_____ 5. Father Kolbe, who was viewed as a threat by the Germans, was arrested in 1941.

_____ 6. He was placed in a concentration camp that held Jews and enemies of the Nazis.

_____ 7. Auschwitz, which was both a labor camp and a death camp, was his destination.

_____ 8. Kolbe was put to work on a building in which people were to be burned to death.

_____ 9. After someone escaped from the camp, the Nazis chose 10 people who would be killed in retribution.

_____ 10. Kolbe offered to take the place of a young father who was chosen to die.

B Decide whether the adjective clause in each sentence is restrictive or nonrestrictive. Rewrite the sentences that contain nonrestrictive clauses, adding commas as needed.

1. Father Kolbe who was meant to starve to death slowly was eventually killed by injection.

_____

2. The men who were condemned to death sang hymns and songs of love.

_____

3. Kolbe's courage and sacrifice which were truly heroic are still remembered.

_____

4. The man whom he replaced as a condemned prisoner attended Kolbe's beatification in 1971.

_____

5. The feast day of Kolbe who was canonized in 1982 is August 14.

_____

106 Adverb Clauses

An **adverb clause** is a dependent clause used as an adverb. An adverb clause modifies a verb, an adjective, or an adverb. It tells *where, when, why, in what way, to what extent or degree,* or *under what condition.* A subordinate conjunction joins an adverb clause to an independent clause.

At Yellowstone National Park, the mud pots, bubbling pools of mud, were formed <u>when steam and gas rose from the ground and changed rock into clay</u>.

A Underline the adverb clause in each sentence. Circle the word(s) it modifies.

1. If you visit the West, you should make a trip to Yellowstone.

2. Because there is so much to do, plan to stay several days.

3. More and more tourists visit as the park's popularity has grown.

4. Because Yellowstone sits on magma, it has geysers and thousands of hot springs.

5. When the major geysers erupt, tourists can watch the boiling water shoot into the air.

6. Geysers have been compared to volcanoes because they are similar.

7. Geysers shoot boiling water, while volcanoes shoot out melted rock.

8. After a geyser has erupted, the water seeps back into the earth.

9. When the minerals in the water dry, you can see beautiful formations.

10. At Yellowstone, bears, elk, and bison roam wherever they want.

11. The balance of nature is maintained even though it sometimes seems cruel.

12. If the park's elk population becomes too large, many animals starve in winter.

13. Feeding animals is prohibited because it alters their natural eating habits.

14. Even though black bears seem friendly, people should avoid them.

15. Before you can camp in the wilderness, you must obtain a permit.

B Use each adverb clause in a sentence.

1. If you stop to think about it, _____ .

2. Until the rain stops, _____ .

3. After I finish my homework, _____ .

4. Although I am good in math, _____ .

5. Since the computer was invented, _____ .

107 More Adverb Clauses

Remember that an adverb clause is always introduced by a subordinate conjunction. Be careful not to confuse a subordinate conjunction with a preposition. A subordinate conjunction connects two complete clauses, but a preposition has only a noun or a pronoun as an object.

SUBORDINATE CONJUNCTION   **We waited <u>until our favorite TV show was on.</u>**

PREPOSITION   **I can hardly wait <u>until tomorrow</u> for Katie's visit.**

A **Complete each sentence with an adverb clause. The subordinate conjunction is given.**

1. We will eat dinner when

   _____ .

2. Jason answered as soon as _____ .

3. He listened to the stereo after _____ .

4. When _____ , the birds fly southward.

5. They return after _____ .

6. The storm arose as soon as _____ .

7. Edward acted as though _____ .

8. Because _____ , I cannot recommend him.

9. He waited until _____ .

10. The expedition struggled on while _____ .

B **Complete each sentence with an adverb clause. Circle each subordinate conjunction.**

1. The pizza finally arrived _____ .

2. School was dismissed _____ .

3. The car broke down on the highway _____ .

4. _____ I ate two hamburgers and a large pickle.

5. _____ the rain ruined the new rug.

6. _____ we drove home from vacation.

7. _____ the milk in the refrigerator was sour.

8. _____ everyone dressed in ratty clothes.

9. _____ I opened my drawer, but there were no socks.

10. _____ Dad made me a delicious club sandwich.

108 Reviewing Adjective Clauses and Adverb Clauses

A Underline the dependent clause in each sentence. On the line write whether it is an adjective clause or an adverb clause.

_____ 1. Before you visit a Florida beach, you should become familiar with its creatures.

_____ 2. People collect seashells because they are beautiful.

_____ 3. Sea urchins, whose spines are sharp, are called the porcupines of the sea.

_____ 4. A sea cucumber is a marine animal that looks like a cucumber.

_____ 5. Until Pam studied seahorses, she didn't realize that the male helps hatch the eggs.

_____ 6. When the ocean tide is low, you can see a variety of sea life.

_____ 7. Sea turtles, which weigh up to 300 pounds, come ashore to lay eggs.

_____ 8. After I was stung by a Portuguese man-of-war, I became more careful.

_____ 9. A blue crab, whose legs really are blue, is a delicacy in the Far East.

_____ 10. If you're hungry, you can make a tasty broth from coquinas.

B Complete each sentence with an adjective clause.

11. Our teacher, _____ , returned the test papers.

12. I enjoyed reading this book, _____ .

13. The players, _____ , did not stop until noon.

14. The car, _____ , broke down.

15. The Joneses, _____ , left the party.

C Complete each sentence with an adverb clause.

16. _____ , we decided to play volleyball.

17. Take the train _____ .

18. I ate everything in sight _____ .

19. _____ , I plan to read four novels.

20. We were stranded on the island _____ .

109 Noun Clauses as Subjects

A **noun clause** is a dependent clause used as a noun. It can perform several functions in a sentence, including serving as the subject. A noun clause is a dependent clause even though it is an essential part of the independent clause.

That reptiles fascinate people is clearly shown in the film. (*That reptiles fascinate people is a subordinate clause; the entire clause serves as the subject of the sentence.*)

A Underline the noun clause used as a subject in each sentence.

1. That pandas are adorable creatures is undisputed.
2. Whether pandas are endangered is also not questioned.
3. Why some pandas reproduce and others don't is being studied.
4. That female pandas can mate for only about three days each year is a biological fact.
5. That pandas are essentially solitary doesn't increase their odds of reproducing.
6. What scientists are learning about pandas in captivity may help keep pandas alive in the wild.
7. That female pandas usually give birth to twins is not new information.
8. Why the mother panda frequently rejects one twin is a puzzle.
9. Whether the female selects the stronger twin is not known.
10. Whoever solves that mystery will help increase the panda population.

B Complete each sentence with a noun clause used as the subject. Remember that a clause has a subject and a predicate.

1. _____ was not clear at all.
2. _____ was perfectly evident.
3. _____ did not discourage him.
4. _____ was a well-kept secret.
5. _____ mystified everyone.
6. _____ will be decided by the group.
7. _____ is clear to most of us.
8. _____ will be announced.
9. _____ was not a surprise to Jay.
10. _____ is the topic of my paper.

110 Noun Clauses as Subject Complements

A noun clause may be used as a subject complement.

The question was whether the candidate had strong views on vital issues.
(*Whether the candidate had strong views on vital issues* is the subject complement; it restates the subject *question*.)

A Underline the noun clause used as a subject complement in each sentence.

1. A qualification for the presidency is that the candidate be a native-born citizen.

2. Is this what you understood about the qualifications?

3. Constant fund-raising is what can take up a candidate's time.

4. The best candidate is not always who will win.

5. Their greatest disappointment is that they don't have time to study the issues.

6. The demand of the voters was that the lottery money be spent on schools.

7. The issue was how test scores could be raised.

8. The decision of the committee was that the money would go for energy research.

9. The senator's prediction was that aid to foreign countries would decrease.

10. A requirement is that the country must improve its human rights record.

B Complete each sentence with a noun clause used as a subject complement. Remember that a clause has a subject and a predicate.

1. A safety rule of biking is _____ .

2. His chief difficulty was _____ .

3. My main concern is _____ .

4. The pilot's first thought was _____ .

5. The advice of our coach is _____ .

6. The survivor's only hope is _____ .

7. The question became _____ .

8. The student's excuse, as always, will be _____ .

9. The reason for the defeat was _____ .

10. Mom's greatest joy was _____ .

111 Noun Clauses as Appositives

A noun clause may be used as an appositive.

The theory that Surtsey is an island created by an underwater volcano intrigues me.
(That Surtsey is an island created by an underwater volcano is an appositive that renames
the noun *theory*.)

A Underline the noun clause used as an appositive in each sentence.
Circle the word it renames.

1. The idea that a new landform can be created seems like science fiction.

2. The fact that an island can be formed from an underground volcanic eruption
   is fantastic.

3. The people of Iceland accepted the idea that an island was growing off their
   southern coast.

4. In class we discussed the idea that eruptions can be divided into six groups.

5. The classification, how scientists identify various volcanoes, is based on
   violence of eruption and material erupted.

6. The fact that the eruption of Mount Pelee in 1902 killed more than
   38,000 people is the reason that most violent eruptions are called Pelean.

7. The promise that we would see an Icelandic eruption came true.

8. My sister's wish that she see a volcano erupt is possible.

9. Dad kept his promise that he would take us to see Kilauea.

10. I find very odd the thought that people want to see
    something so destructive.

B Complete each sentence with a noun clause used as an appositive. Remember that a
clause has a subject and a predicate.

1. Joan kept her promise _____ .

2. The motion _____ .

3. The rumor _____ .

4. Her suggestion _____ .

5. The fear _____ .

6. Trudy was upset by the report _____ .

7. The thought _____ .

8. Dad's wish _____ .

9. My idea _____ .

10. Jack's assumption _____ .

Sentences

112 Noun Clauses as Direct Objects

A noun clause may be used as the direct object of a verb.

Scientists know <u>that the balance in nature is easily upset</u>.

(That the balance in nature is easily upset is the direct object of the verb *know.)*

A **Underline the noun clause used as the direct object.**

1. We know that all parts of an ecosystem are important.

2. Did you realize that harvesting a species of crab can lead to a decline in a species of bird?

3. Biologists know that horseshoe crabs come ashore in Delaware Bay to spawn in May.

4. They also know that shorebirds arrive to eat crabs' eggs.

5. The crabs' eggs provide whatever energy the birds have for their migration to the Arctic.

6. Lately biologists have noticed that the number of red knots, a type of shorebird, has declined.

7. Scientists think that the birds' food supply has dwindled.

8. They believe that commercial fishing is responsible for the decline in the number of crabs.

9. They have calculated that half the crab population in Delaware Bay is gone.

10. The U.S. Department of Commerce proposed that we set aside an area in the ocean as a horseshoe-crab reserve.

B **Complete each sentence with a noun clause used as the direct object. Remember that a clause has a subject and a predicate.**

1. The boy said _____ .

2. She could not remember _____ .

3. We all knew _____ .

4. Our teacher promised _____ .

5. Did they discover _____ ?

6. Kim proved _____ .

7. We should always do _____ .

8. Has anyone heard _____ ?

9. Jerry tried to explain _____ .

10. All of us hope _____ .

113 Noun Clauses as Objects of Prepositions

A noun clause may be used as the object of a preposition.

The spectators came upon <u>what was an ancient racetrack.</u>

(What was an ancient racetrack is the object of the preposition upon.)

A Underline the noun clause used as the object of a preposition. Circle the preposition.

1. We had an excellent view of the race from where we stood.

2. We searched through what used to be Grandma's old chest.

3. Last week the team studied about how the previous relay teams trained.

4. The group walked around where the old town plaza had been.

5. During the summer I practiced my shots in what is the renovated recreation center.

6. The bridge passes over where the rivers meet.

7. The bug crawled under whatever was lying on the table.

8. John gave every explanation except why he was so late.

9. You give the baton to whoever is there.

10. Our coach will give a pizza to whoever wins the heat.

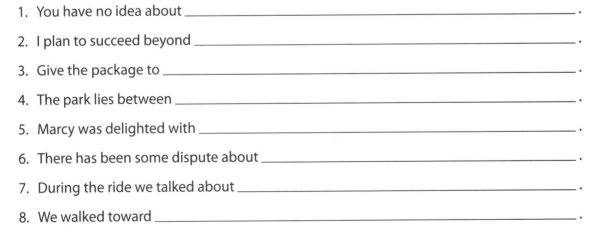

B Complete each sentence with a noun clause used as the object of the preposition. The preposition to use is given. Remember that a clause has a subject and a predicate.

1. You have no idea about _____ .

2. I plan to succeed beyond _____ .

3. Give the package to _____ .

4. The park lies between _____ .

5. Marcy was delighted with _____ .

6. There has been some dispute about _____ .

7. During the ride we talked about _____ .

8. We walked toward _____ .

9. Many books have been written about _____ .

10. She can give the assignment to _____ .

114 Reviewing Noun Clauses

A Underline the noun clause in each sentence. Write on the line how it is used. Use **S** for subject, **DO** for direct object, **OP** for object of a preposition, **SC** for subject complement, and **APP** for appositive.

_____ 1. This article says that a society lived in Peru a thousand years before the Inca.

_____ 2. Such a discovery is exciting to whoever is interested in archaeology.

_____ 3. The truth is that the Moche state extended 220 miles along Peru's coast.

_____ 4. That the Moche had a highly stratified society is indicated by the burial tombs.

_____ 5. Excavations, where archaeologists clear away tons of rock and dirt, are yielding fabulous objects of gold, silver, and copper.

_____ 6. That these tombs were looted for more than four centuries is unfortunate.

_____ 7. Archaeologists say that the Moche did not have a writing system.

_____ 8. Whatever we know about their activities is recorded on ceramic pots, textiles, and murals.

_____ 9. The fact is that the Moche lived in one of the driest regions on earth.

_____ 10. Archaeologists say that the Moche had a complicated irrigation system.

_____ 11. One idea is that bats were important symbols to the Moche.

_____ 12. Archaeologists explain that bats appear in depictions of human sacrifice.

_____ 13. One find, what appeared to be a headdress with bats, supports this theory.

_____ 14. A fact about each burial tomb is that it contained one very tall adult male.

_____ 15. Archaeologists do not know why such a man was buried with much smaller people.

B Write sentences, using each noun clause as indicated.

16. that those children study *(direct object)*

_____

17. when the Yankees won the World Series *(subject)*

_____

18. whether the clock is correct *(subject complement)*

_____

19. whatever dangers threatened it *(object of a preposition)*

_____

20. that she was running for mayor *(appositive)*

_____

115 Reviewing Clauses

A Underline the subordinate clause in each sentence.
Write whether it is used as an adjective, an adverb, or a noun.

_____ 1. Smokey Bear, who became a fire-prevention symbol, was rescued from a fire 60 years ago.

_____ 2. A bear cub is a creature that everybody loves.

_____ 3. After the cub was rescued from the fire in New Mexico, he was sent to a zoo.

_____ 4. As a fire raged through Montana in 2000, another cub was found.

_____ 5. The cub, which was a black bear, was found by a game warden.

_____ 6. The cub needed help because his little paws were burned.

_____ 7. What the rescuers should do with this cub after bandaging his paws was not an issue.

_____ 8. A wildlife official insisted that this cub go back to the forest.

_____ 9. The plan was that the cub be put into a hand-dug den to hibernate.

_____ 10. The cub was in the den with another orphaned cub that rangers found.

B Combine each set of sentences into one sentence, using an adjective clause or an adverb clause as directed. Use a subordinate conjunction to connect clauses.

11. *(adverb)* Traffic was backed up for miles. A huge truck was on fire.

_____

_____

12. *(adverb)* I turned the corner. A gust of wind blew my hat off.

_____

_____

13. *(adjective)* Leonardo da Vinci made a mechanical lion. Leonardo da Vinci was an artist and inventor.

_____

_____

14. *(adverb)* I was standing in a good spot. I had an excellent view of the Grand Canyon.

_____

_____

115 Reviewing Clauses, continued

15. *(adjective)* There are magazines piled on the table. Don't take any of the magazines.

_____

_____

16. *(adjective)* The Battle of New Orleans was fought in January 1815. It lasted only 20 minutes.

_____

_____

17. *(adverb)* John and Sue did all the work. We should be grateful to John and Sue.

_____

_____

18. *(adverb)* Frank was vice president of the camera club. Frank organized many interesting programs.

_____

_____

19. *(adjective)* A new supermarket is opening here soon. The supermarket will provide jobs for many people.

_____

_____

20. *(adverb)* The skaters finally arrived home. They were cold, tired, and hungry.

_____

_____

C Write sentences, using these noun clauses as indicated.

21. where they had started *(object of a preposition)*

_____

22. that the contest be held at this school *(subject complement)*

_____

23. whether I will arrive in time *(subject)*

_____

24. that we visit my aunt *(appositive)*

_____

25. where the game was being played *(direct object)*

_____

_____

116 Simple Sentences

A **simple sentence** consists of one independent clause. Remember that an independent clause has a subject and a predicate and can stand alone as a complete thought.

A Make sentences by matching the complete subjects in Column A with the complete predicates in Column B. Write the correct letter on the line. Use each letter once.

COLUMN A

_____ 1. A cat's skeleton

_____ 2. The exact number of bones

_____ 3. The skeleton

_____ 4. A cat's ears

_____ 5. After eating or sleeping, a cat

_____ 6. Long, thin, flexible leg muscles

_____ 7. Owners sometimes

_____ 8. Being a carnivore, a cat

_____ 9. A cat's tail

_____ 10. Pads on its paws

COLUMN B

a. has about 250 bones.

b. aid in a soft landing.

c. helps it stay balanced.

d. depends on tail length.

e. protects internal organs.

f. cleans itself.

g. enable a cat to run fast.

h. can lie flat on its head.

i. remove a cat's claws.

j. likes to eat meat.

B Choose the best simple predicate to complete each sentence. Use each once.

have written	read	borrowed	describes	named
imagined	enjoy	saw	appears	delights

1. Authors throughout the ages _____ about cats.

2. *Puss in Boots* _____ both young and old readers.

3. A favorite nursery rhyme _____ mittenless kittens.

4. The author of *Catwings* _____ flying cats.

5. In *Alice in Wonderland,* a Cheshire cat _____ from time to time.

6. We _____ a play about Dick Whittington and his cat.

7. I _____ a book about a cat that saw ghosts.

8. I _____ reading poetry about cats.

9. Sometimes I _____ aloud to my cat, Jake.

10. My sister _____ her black cat Ichabod Crane.

Sentences

117 Compound Sentences

A **compound sentence** contains two or more independent clauses. The clauses may be joined in three different ways.

The day was cold, yet we decided to go. (comma and conjunction)

The day was cold; we still decided to go. (semicolon)

The day was cold; nevertheless, we decided to go.
(semicolon and adverb)

A Create compound sentences by combining clauses from both columns. Use each clause once. On the line at the left, write the letter of your selection from Column B. On the line at the right, add the proper punctuation and, as appropriate, a conjunction or an adverb.

COLUMN A

_____ 1. Cars are easy to drive _____

_____ 2. Dad bought a new SUV _____

_____ 3. We like riding in it _____

_____ 4. The car is good for off-road driving _____

_____ 5. Mom does not drive _____

_____ 6. She walks everywhere _____

_____ 7. Riding a bike is good exercise _____

_____ 8. My sister is 16 _____

_____ 9. Will she pay for gas _____

_____ 10. Fuel prices go up _____

COLUMN B

a. will Dad pay?

b. they are expensive to maintain.

c. does she want to.

d. people still want to drive.

e. she wants to drive.

f. it doesn't pollute.

g. she rides her bicycle.

h. we live in a suburb.

i. we don't enjoy buying gas for it.

j. it uses a lot of fuel.

B Complete each sentence with an independent clause.

1. The girls arranged the chairs, and _____ .

2. The assignment was difficult, but _____ .

3. The crowd was silent; _____ .

4. Finally the game began, and _____ .

5. Take my advice, and _____ .

6. I am not a musician, but _____ .

7. The weeds we pulled were poison ivy; consequently, _____ .

8. I did not finish my chores; therefore, _____ .

9. We spent the entire afternoon at the beach, and _____ .

10. We bought treats for the children, but _____ .

118 Complex Sentences

A **complex sentence** contains one independent and one or more dependent clauses.

DEPENDENT CLAUSE   **INDEPENDENT CLAUSE**
If you visit Australia,   **you can see the largest coral reef in the world.**

A   Underline the independent clause in each sentence. Write the word that begins each dependent clause on the line.

_____ 1. Although the name suggests a continuous strip, Australia's Great Barrier Reef is made up of more than 2,800 reefs.

_____ 2. A coral reef forms when colonies of plant and animal skeletons pile up.

_____ 3. Divers meet many sharks that seem more curious than dangerous.

_____ 4. Because the waters are clear, divers can go 150 feet deep or lower.

_____ 5. Biologists, who find new species of fish every year, have already discovered more than 2,000.

B   Underline the dependent clause in each sentence. Write the word that begins each dependent clause on the line.

_____ 1. Because they look like plants, corals were originally wrongly classified.

_____ 2. After corals were studied further, scientists likened them to anemones and jellyfish.

_____ 3. Because they eat other animals, corals are carnivores.

_____ 4. If you dive around the Great Barrier Reef, you are likely to see sea turtles.

_____ 5. Some marks on a sea turtle's shell are from sharks that bit it.

C   Complete each sentence with a dependent clause.

1. Vegetables are good for you _____.

2. The dog panted as _____.

3. July 4 is the date _____.

4. I have a suggestion _____.

5. We wondered it worked _____.

6. Spring is the season _____.

7. We should honor our school _____.

8. Be sure to return those books _____.

9. I will finish my paper _____.

10. The game was forfeited _____.

119 Combining Sentences

A simple sentence consists of a subject and a predicate, either of which may be compound. A compound sentence consists of two or more independent clauses. A complex sentence contains one independent clause and one or more dependent clauses.

Combine each pair of sentences. Write at least two simple sentences, two compound sentences, and two complex sentences. After each of your sentences, write whether it is simple, compound, or complex.

1. The date of the festivities was announced. I cannot attend.

   _____

   _____

2. Books are a great source of knowledge. They can broaden people's minds.

   _____

   _____

3. Football is an exciting sport. I like hockey more than football.

   _____

   _____

4. Snakes are unusual animals. They are often misunderstood.

   _____

   _____

5. The car sped around the corner. It skidded into a ditch.

   _____

   _____

6. Study in a quiet place. You will be able to concentrate.

   _____

   _____

7. The students assemble in the yard. They assemble there every morning.

   _____

   _____

8. The aircraft carrier entered the harbor. People on the dock cheered.

   _____

   _____

9. The students were cooperative all year. The class went on a trip to a theme park.

   _____

   _____

10. The story is quite interesting. It was written by Walter Dean Myers.

    _____

    _____

120 Reviewing Sentences

A Tell how each underlined phrase is used. Write **PREP** if it is a prepositional phrase, **PART** if a participle, **INF** if an infinitive, or **GER** if a gerund.

_____ 1. *Mary Rose,* an English ship <u>built in the early 1500s</u>, sank in 1545 near the southern coast of England.

_____ 2. The story <u>of this famous shipwreck</u> is fascinating.

_____ 3. <u>Recovering the ship</u> was a painstaking task.

_____ 4. The effort <u>to raise the ship</u> was successful in 1982.

_____ 5. It was watched on TV <u>by some 60 million people</u>.

B Underline the dependent clause in each sentence.

6. When the *Mary Rose* was built, it was one of the first warships with cannons on its sides.

7. People of the time said that it was a favorite ship of King Henry VIII.

8. The king was actually present as the ship went out to sea in 1545.

9. A storm that arose very suddenly sank the ship.

10. Although most of the crew was lost, some of them did survive.

11. The *Mary Rose* settled into the silt on the ocean floor, which helped preserve it over the centuries.

12. That the ship remained intact for so many years was truly amazing.

13. The objects that were recovered from the ship present a view into the world of the 1500s.

14. From the remains, historians have learned about what sailors at that time ate.

15. Archaeologists have even found leather shoes that survived all those years in the water.

C Underline the dependent clause in each sentence. Write **ADJ** if it is used as an adjective, **ADV** if used as an adverb, or **N** if used as a noun.

_____ 16. Because the ship contained so many artifacts, historians have learned a lot about its crew.

_____ 17. The games that were found include a backgammon board with pieces.

_____ 18. That music was important in a sailor's life is obvious from the number of musical instruments on board.

_____ 19. The amount of fishing equipment found indicates that fishing was a major pastime for the sailors.

_____ 20. The leather covers of some books survived although the pages of the books had deteriorated.

_____ 21. A chest that had containers in it belonged to the ship's surgeon-barber.

_____ 22. It contained peppercorns, which were used as a medicine at the time.

Continued →

120 Reviewing Sentences, *continued*

_____ 23. When crew members were injured, the surgeon tended to them.

_____ 24. At other times he groomed sailors who wished to be shaved.

_____ 25. That there was little gold aboard the warship was not surprising.

D Identify the type of each sentence by writing *simple, compound,* or *complex.*

_____ 26. The *Mary Rose* is now in a museum in Portsmouth, England.

_____ 27. Visitors may actually touch a piece of rope that was under the sea for more than 400 years.

_____ 28. For a period of time after the wooden ship was raised, it was preserved by a constant spray of water.

_____ 29. The ship is now being coated with a water-soluble wax polyethylene to help preserve it.

_____ 30. This process will be completed in several years, and the ship will then go through a drying process.

Try It Yourself

On a separate sheet of paper, write five or six sentences about an animal you would like to study. Vary your writing by including different kinds of sentences.

Check Your Own Work

Choose a selection from your writing portfolio, a journal, a work in progress, an assignment from another class, or a letter. Revise it, applying the skills you have reviewed. This checklist will help you.

✔ Have you varied your sentences, using simple, compound, and complex sentences when appropriate?

✔ Have you combined sentence parts correctly?

121 Coordinating Conjunctions

A **conjunction** is a word used to connect words or groups of words. A **coordinating conjunction** joins words or groups of words that are similar. It can also connect independent clauses to form compound sentences. The coordinating conjunctions are *and, but, or, nor, so,* and *yet.*

Elizabeth I ruled England and Ireland. (words)

Her reign was troubled by religious unrest at home and by tensions with continental powers. (phrases)

The political achievements during her reign were impressive, but the artistic achievements also were impressive. (clauses)

Circle the coordinating conjunction in each sentence. Underline the words or group of words it joins. On the line write **W** if it joins words, **P** if it joins phrases, and **C** if it joins clauses.

_____ 1. Elizabeth's reign lasted more than four decades, and she is considered one of England's most famous rulers.

_____ 2. There were great achievements and prosperity during her reign.

_____ 3. She ruled England from 1558 to 1603, so this period is commonly referred to as the Elizabethan Age.

_____ 4. This was a time for the English nation and for English arts to flourish.

_____ 5. Elizabethan dramatists include Shakespeare and Christopher Marlowe.

_____ 6. Elizabeth became queen, but she had had a difficult childhood.

_____ 7. She was locked in the Tower of London for two months, and she was threatened with execution.

_____ 8. Elizabeth earlier had supported her sister Mary's becoming queen, yet Mary had her imprisoned.

_____ 9. Elizabeth was young at the start of her reign, but she ruled with great intelligence.

_____ 10. She had grown into a striking young lady who did not use cosmetics or wear fancy clothes.

_____ 11. During her reign the English navy defeated the Spanish Armada, so England became a great sea power.

_____ 12. This helped the nation's merchants and its economy.

_____ 13. England prospered despite foreign threats and despite religious unrest.

_____ 14. Elizabeth was dedicated to her country and to her people.

_____ 15. Her reign is noted for its poets and dramatists.

Queen Elizabeth I was a supporter of writers, artists, and musicians. Describe a way you can encourage the creativity of others.

122 Correlative Conjunctions

Correlative conjunctions are conjunctions that are used in pairs to connect words or groups of words that have parallel structure in a sentence. The most commonly used correlative conjunctions are *both . . . and, either . . . or, neither . . . nor, not only . . . but also,* and *whether . . . or.*

Circle the correlative conjunctions in each sentence. Underline the words or phrases they connect.

1. Historians think Native Americans crossed over from Asia either as late as 12,000 years ago or as early as 40,000 years ago.

2. Whether at the earlier date or at the later date, they probably came from Siberia.

3. Early Americans were both hunters and farmers.

4. Native Americans lived either in permanent houses or in portable ones.

5. Some had not only winter homes but also summer homes.

6. Many lived in either towns or small villages.

7. Native Americans wore clothes of either animal skin or plant fiber.

8. Because these Native Americans had neither horses nor oxen, they often traveled by water in canoes.

9. Both corn and beans, which could be stored and dried, were important in the diet of Native Americans in the East.

10. These crops were rich not only in protein but also in essential vitamins.

11. Both beans and squash were often planted in the same field as corn.

12. The squash served both to choke weeds and to keep the ground moist.

13. Different groups of Native Americans worshiped different gods, some of which were either the sun or animals like buffalo.

14. Religious leaders called shamans had the power not only to contact the spirit world but also to help in healing.

15. A shaman might use both spiritual power and herbal medicines in treating an illness.

16. Both men and women were usually involved in providing food, but they would likely have had different tasks.

17. Europeans had neither corn nor tomatoes before their arrival in the Americas.

18. Neither horses nor sheep were known to Native Americans before Europeans arrived.

19. Both the Native Americans and the Europeans changed because of their contact with each other in North America.

20. Some regional cultures embrace not only European but also Native American ways.

123 Conjunctive Adverbs

A **conjunctive adverb** connects independent clauses and helps make their relationship clear. Some common conjunctive adverbs are *also, besides, consequently, however, in fact, later, moreover, nevertheless, otherwise, still,* and *therefore.* When a conjunctive adverb connects clauses, a semicolon is used before it and a comma after it.

A **Underline the conjunctive adverb in each sentence.**

1. One of the most famous diamonds in the world is a large blue diamond with a reddish tint called the Hope Diamond; indeed, it has a fascinating history.
2. A merchant bought a 112-carat diamond in India; later, he sold it to King Louis XIV.
3. The diamond became part of the French crown jewels; in fact, the king himself wore it.
4. During the French Revolution, King Louis XVI tried to flee with the jewels; consequently, the revolutionary government seized them.
5. Later the jewels were stolen, and people thought they had been lost forever; however, in 1812 a 45-carat blue diamond appeared on the English market.

B **Combine each pair of sentences into a single compound sentence. Choose the correct conjunctive adverb in parentheses. Add semicolons and commas as needed.**

1. The thieves would not have wanted to get caught. (Therefore Moreover) they would likely have had the diamond cut again to alter its appearance.

   _____

   _____

2. The Hope Diamond is smaller than the original diamond. (Still Moreover) it is striking.

   _____

   _____

3. One of its owners was named Hope. (Nevertheless Consequently) it was given that name.

   _____

   _____

4. The Hope Diamond had several other owners. (Finally Therefore) it became part of a collection at the Smithsonian Institution in Washington, D.C.

   _____

   _____

5. Recent research seems to confirm that the Hope Diamond was cut from the lost French diamond. (However In fact) some of its sides may even be the same.

   _____

   _____

8 | Conjunctions & Interjections

124 Subordinate Conjunctions

A **subordinate conjunction** is used to join an independent clause and a dependent clause and to indicate their relationship. Subordinate conjunctions generally introduce adverb clauses. Common subordinate conjunctions are *after, although, because, before, even though, if, in order that, since, so that, than, when,* and *while.*

INDEPENDENT CLAUSE	SUBORDINATE CONJUNCTION IN THE DEPENDENT CLAUSE
Ludwig wanted to practice	**even though his elbow ached.**

A Circle each subordinate conjunction. Underline each dependent clause.

1. Although she is fictitious, Rosie the Riveter played an important role in World War II.

2. Before the war started, most American women did not work outside their homes.

3. Many jobs were left vacant, however, when men began enlisting in the army.

4. Because a war was being fought, production of certain goods had to be increased.

5. Something had to be done so that America's productivity did not decline during the war.

6. Since help was needed to maintain production, an ad campaign was designed to recruit women.

7. Rosie the Riveter was created in order that women would view factory work as patriotic.

8. Before the war was over, more than six million women had joined the workforce.

9. The needs of Americans would not have been met if it had not been for their help.

10. Although many lost their jobs after the war, these women helped make working outside the home acceptable.

B Write sentences, using the following dependent clauses.

because it was cold inside   1. _____

if we are going   2. _____

unless we hear otherwise   3. _____

although it was raining   4. _____

so that everyone gets a turn   5. _____

Conjunctions & Interjections   8

125 Troublesome Conjunctions

Some conjunctions are frequently confused with prepositions. *Without* is a preposition; it helps form a prepositional phrase. *Unless* is a subordinate conjunction; it introduces an adverb clause.

They will be lost <u>without</u> a map.

They will get lost <u>unless</u> you go with them.

Like is a preposition. *As if* is a subordinate conjunction used to introduce an adverb clause. *As* can function as a preposition or a conjunction.

Animals <u>like</u> zebras and cheetahs appear in my favorite nature films.

Sometimes I act <u>as if</u> I am on a safari, preparing to shoot a movie.

My brother, <u>as</u> the movie's director, likes to order me around.

<u>As</u> we move across the jungle in our backyard, I can just see the wild animals.

A Circle the correct word in parentheses.

1. You won't see a camel in America (unless without) you go to a zoo.
2. Camels have been introduced to America but (unless without) success.
3. They can bear severe heat (like as if) it were nothing.
4. Camels can go (without unless) water for several days.
5. They can also drink salt water (without unless) getting sick.
6. Many people think a camel's hump acts (as as if) a storage area.
7. The hump actually contains fat that is absorbed (like as) the camel needs energy.
8. During sandstorms a camel's nostrils can close (like as) shutters do.
9. A camel, (as like) a giraffe, runs with both legs on one side moving at the same time.
10. I would not want to cross a desert (without unless) I had a camel.

B Complete each sentence with the correct word: ***without, unless, as,*** or ***like.***

1. _____ a fire moves across land, it usually kills the vegetation in its path.
2. One type of protea flower cannot survive, however, _____ fire.
3. Seeds _____ large nuts remain in the flower head for a year.
4. _____ the plant is scorched by fire, it will not release its seeds.
5. _____ the fire passes, the bracts open, and the protea seeds are released.
6. The plant will retain the seeds until it dies _____ there is a fire.
7. Fire permits sunlight to reach small plants _____ it destroys large shade trees.
8. The ashes also act _____ fertilizer for the soil.
9. _____ these advantages the protea would have difficulty surviving.
10. So the fire, _____ a sign, tells the plant that it is OK to release its seeds.

126 Interjections

An **interjection** is a word that expresses a strong or sudden emotion, such as delight, anger, surprise, anticipation, warning, impatience, pain, or wonder. An interjection may be set off from the rest of a sentence by an exclamation point. It may also function as part of an exclamatory sentence; if so, it is followed by a comma.

Ouch! The sand is hot.

Wow, the view from here is incredible!

A Underline the interjection. Write on the line what emotion it expresses.

_____ 1. Listen! You can hear the waves crashing on the beach.

_____ 2. Hello! Is anyone at home?

_____ 3. Careful! The lifeguard said there is an undertow.

_____ 4. Goodness! This mattress must be filled with rocks.

_____ 5. Quiet! The baby is sleeping.

_____ 6. See, that is what happens when you leave milk out overnight!

_____ 7. Look! There are dolphins playing in the water.

_____ 8. Oh! I did not know anyone was in here.

_____ 9. Enough, that really hurts!

_____ 10. Hey! No pets are allowed in the museum.

B Write a sentence, using an interjection to express each emotion.

pain 1. _____

joy 2. _____

assent 3. _____

disgust 4. _____

wonder 5. _____

impatience 6. _____

surprise 7. _____

sorrow 8. _____

warning 9. _____

delight 10. _____

127 Reviewing Conjunctions & Interjections

A On the line describe the italicized word(s) by writing **A** for a coordinating conjunction, **B** for correlative conjunctions, **C** for a subordinate conjunction, or **D** for a conjunctive adverb.

_____ 1. *Although* its name implies something else, the Dead Sea is actually a lake.

_____ 2. It does sustain life forms; *therefore*, it is not really dead.

_____ 3. Fish cannot live in its salty water; *however*, some salt-loving microorganisms thrive there.

_____ 4. Scientists have discovered that these microorganisms *not only* cope *but also* become addicted to the salt.

_____ 5. The Dead Sea contains seven times more salt *than* seawater contains.

_____ 6. Nearly a third of the lake consists of salt *and* other solid minerals.

_____ 7. *Because* the water is so dense, a human body can float easily on its surface.

_____ 8. The Dead Sea is fed by the Jordan River *and* several smaller streams.

_____ 9. The lake has no outlet; *consequently*, water is carried off solely by evaporation.

_____ 10. The ruins of *both* Sodom *and* Gomorrah, ancient Biblical cities, are believed to lie beneath the lake.

B Underline the coordinating conjunction, correlative conjunction, subordinate conjunction, or conjunctive adverb in each sentence. On the line identify the words you underlined, using the letters from Exercise A.

_____ 11. Lake Baikal was formed about 25 million years ago; therefore, it is believed to be the world's oldest lake.

_____ 12. Because the lake lies far north in Siberia, it is frozen from January to May.

_____ 13. About 335 rivers and streams flow into Lake Baikal, but only one flows out.

_____ 14. Both parks and nature reserves lie along the lake's shore.

_____ 15. Lake Baikal is the deepest lake in the world; in fact, it contains about 20 percent of the world's unfrozen fresh water.

_____ 16. Lake Baikal has about 15,000 species unique to it; therefore, it has been compared to the Galapagos Islands off South America.

_____ 17. Lake Baikal is visited and studied by many scientists.

_____ 18. The unusual wildlife of the lake includes a fish called golomyanka and a freshwater seal called the Baikal seal.

_____ 19. Although attempts are being made to preserve the lake, there is increasing pollution.

_____ 20. Neither the water nor the air in the area has retained the degree of cleanliness it had in the recent past.

8 | Conjunctions & Interjections

Continued →

127 **Reviewing Conjunctions & Interjections,** *continued*

C Circle the coordinating conjunction or the correlative conjunction. Underline the word or groups of words that the conjunction connects.

21. Both the Dead Sea and the Great Salt Lake are very salty.

22. Neither the Dead Sea nor the Great Salt Lake has any outflowing streams.

23. The Great Salt Lake is fed by three major rivers and rainfall.

24. Several minor streams flow into the Great Salt Lake, but none flows out.

25. The lake is enjoyed not only by swimmers but also by boaters.

D Circle each subordinate conjunction. Underline each dependent clause.

26. The Great Salt Lake has been divided into north and south sections since a railroad causeway was constructed through it in 1959.

27. After I read about the lake, I wanted to visit it.

28. The salt remains in the Great Salt Lake when evaporation occurs.

E Complete each sentence with an appropriate conjunctive adverb.

29. Visitors can swim or boat on the lake; _____ , they can visit a state park.

30. The waters in the northern part of the lake are extremely salty; _____ , only salt-loving algae and bacteria live there.

31. Few organisms exist in the northern part of the lake; _____ , the southern part has shrimp and flies on which birds feed.

F Add an appropriate interjection to each item.

32. _____ You finally got to visit the Great Salt Lake.

33. _____ What happened to all your photos?

34. _____ You got to see buffalo on the island.

35. _____ You didn't get to float on the lake.

Try It Yourself

On a separate sheet of paper, write about some places that you would like to visit and what you would see there.

Check Your Own Work

Choose a selection from your writing portfolio, a journal, a work in progress, an assignment from another class, or a letter. Revise it, applying the skills you have reviewed. This checklist will help you.

✔ Have you used conjunctions correctly?

✔ Do the coordinating conjunctions and correlative conjunctions connect words or phrases that are parallel in form?

128 Periods

A **period** is used

- at the end of a declarative or an imperative sentence

  You read *The Golden Compass.*
  Tell me about the book.

- after most abbreviations, such as titles and standard measurements (but not metric measurements)

Gov.	**Governor**	**a.m.**	**before noon**
St.	**Street**	**Feb.**	**February**
Inc.	**Incorporated**	**pt.**	**pint**

- after the initials in a name

F. D. Roosevelt	**Franklin Delano Roosevelt**
T. A. Edison	**Thomas Alva Edison**

A Rewrite the following phrases, substituting abbreviations and adding periods as appropriate.

1. Patricia A Vogel, MD _____

2. 4 yards _____

3. Tuesday, January 11, 2006 _____

4. Doctor Martin Luther King, Junior _____

5. 147 East Lincoln Avenue _____

B Add periods where needed in the following sentences.

1. Janet S Anderson's *Going Through the Gate* is a suspenseful fantasy with an unusual teacher as a main character

2. Everyone in my class has read at least one of J K Rowling's Harry Potter books

3. S E Hinton's *The Outsiders* is the story of three children trying to stay together after their parents' death

4. Ernest J Gaines's *The Autobiography of Miss Jane Pittman* tells the story of an African American woman and the U S civil rights movement from the time of the Civil War to the 1960s

5. *Don't Sweat the Small Stuff* by Richard Carlson, Ph D, is a self-help book

6. Our librarian, Mr Robertson, recommended that we read J R R Tolkien's *The Lord of the Rings*

7. Dr Seuss was the pen name of Theodor Seuss Geisel, who wrote many popular books for young children

8. Robert C O'Brien's *The Silver Crown* is a book I've read several times

9. There are several poems in English and in Spanish by Francisco X Alarcon in our literature anthology

10. Mrs. Harding assigned us to read two of O Henry's short stories

129 Commas–Part I

Commas are used to separate words in a series of three or more and to separate adjectives of equal importance in front of a noun.

> **Yellowstone National Park, the Grand Canyon, and Niagara Falls are a few of America's natural wonders.**
>
> **A tall, powerful, steamy gush of water in the air means a geyser is erupting.**

A **Add commas where needed.**

1. Yellowstone National Park is located in Idaho Montana and Wyoming.

2. The geology of the area was affected by an ancient volcanic eruption that sent ash over all of the western United States much of the Midwest and northern Mexico.

3. The volcanic magma under the surface of the earth is the cause of the geysers hot springs and muddy pools that rise to the surface of the land.

4. In 1871 an expedition that included the geologist Ferdinand Hayden the artist Thomas Moran and the photographer William Henry Jackson helped convince Congress to make Yellowstone a national park.

5. A special program teaches students about the history of the park investigates issues related to the park's ecosystem and promotes preservation of the park.

6. Old Faithful Castle and Giantess are three of the geysers in the park.

7. The bubbly steamy muddy pools in the park are called mudpots.

8. A mountain of black glass formed by lava a petrified forest and terraces of falling water are among the unusual features of the park.

9. Trumpeter swans white pelicans and blue herons feed in its lakes and rivers.

10. The park has canyons mountains forests and meadows.

B **Rewrite the following sentences to show the correct use of commas. Not all the sentences are incorrect.**

1. Visitors can ride horses, hike and even ski at Yellowstone.

   _____

2. Waterfalls, lakes, and geysers are some of the attractions of the park.

   _____

3. Wildlife in the park includes bears, elk and buffalo.

   _____

4. Buffalo live, roam and graze, in the park.

   _____

5. Rangers naturalists, and a maintenance staff work in the park.

   _____

130 Commas–Part II

A comma is used

- to set off words in direct address

    Have you ever experienced a tropical storm, Rita?

- to set off parts of addresses, place names, and dates

    The concert was held at Madison Square Garden in New York, New York.

    October 15, 2003, was a memorable day in Justin's life.

- after the salutation in a friendly letter and after the complimentary close in all letters

    Dear Ginny,   Very truly yours,

A **Add commas where needed in this e-mail.**

January 8 20—

Dear Elena

　　My cousin works at the National Hurricane Center in Miami Florida. When we visit there, she's going to arrange for us to tour the center. Do you want to come with me and my family? Our tour is scheduled for February 11 20— unless there is a change of date.
　　Write soon and let me know!

Your friend
Arianna

B **Add commas where they are needed.**

1. Can you tell me what a hurricane is class?

2. Did you know that one of the worst weather disasters in U.S. history was a hurricane that hit Galveston Texas?

3. The hurricane struck on September 8 1900.

4. Frederick, more than 6,000 people died in the terrible storm and the huge wave that followed it.

5. Another fierce hurricane took place in 1969 Jackie.

6. It was a hurricane named Camille that struck land on August 17 1969.

7. Louis more than 27 inches of rain fell on parts of Virginia in less than 24 hours in the aftermath of that hurricane.

8. The World Meteorological Organization in Geneva Switzerland names hurricanes.

9. The National Hurricane Center, which gives tours, is located at the following address:
National Hurricane Center
11691 S. W. 17th Street
Miami FL 33165

10. Camp Springs Maryland is the home office of the National Weather Service.

131 Commas–Part III

Commas are used to set off nonrestrictive phrases and clauses. Nonrestrictive phrases are not necessary to the meaning of a sentence; they provide additional information.

> **Washington, D.C., the nation's capital, has many famous monuments.**
>
> **The Washington Monument, which stands on the Mall, is perhaps the most famous monument in the capital.**

A **Add commas to set off nonrestrictive phrases and clauses.**

1. One of the most powerful of all monuments in Washington, D.C., is the Vietnam Memorial which honors the dead U.S. military personnel from the Vietnam War.

2. The war which took place in the 1960s and 1970s divided the American public.

3. In 1981 a committee which consisted of architects and designers selected the best plan for the monument from many entries.

4. The winning entry was from Maya Lin a 21-year-old student at Yale.

5. The design which is basically a polished black granite slab has the names of more than 58,000 men and women carved into it.

6. The Vietnam Memorial now one of the most frequently visited memorials in the United States is considered striking by most people.

7. Lin today a respected architect has her own design studio in New York.

8. Lin who has designed structures in many cities continues to produce original works.

9. Her designs which include buildings and memorials are much sought after.

10. The Civil Rights Memorial a monument in Alabama honoring those who died in the struggle for civil rights was designed by Lin.

B **Rewrite the following sentences, adding commas where necessary. Not all sentences are incorrect.**

1. Maya Lin a famous architect and designer was born in Ohio in 1960.

   _____

2. Lin a Chinese American, takes inspiration from many sources.

   _____

3. These sources, which include Japanese gardens and Native American tombs, are varied.

   _____

4. Her buildings and monuments which are usually specific to a given site are often dramatic.

   _____

5. My family's next vacation a trip to one of Lin's recent monuments was my suggestion.

   _____

132 Commas–Part IV

Commas are used before coordinating conjunctions when they are used to connect two independent clauses to form a compound sentence and after conjunctive adverbs in compound sentences.

Petra is an ancient city, and it is now a World Heritage site.

Petra was long abandoned; therefore, its monuments lay undisturbed for centuries.

A **Add commas where needed.**

1. Petra is an ancient city in Jordan but it has long been abandoned.

2. The city was carved from rose-colored rock; consequently its site is quite beautiful.

3. Petra was in a central location in the Middle East; therefore it became a trading center.

4. Petra prospered from farming; moreover it was on a main caravan route.

5. The city could be reached only through a narrow pass; consequently it was easy to defend.

6. Petra was noted for its complex irrigation system and its builders are considered geniuses for how they made the most of an average yearly rainfall of only six inches.

7. Petra flourished from 400 to 100 BC but it was conquered by Roman troops in AD 106.

8. Many of the buildings in Petra are tombs; however no bodies have been found in them.

9. The walls of the tombs at Petra are dramatically colored magenta and blue and their interiors are truly works of art.

10. These colorful walls were not painted by humans; in fact their dramatic colors result from the natural colors of the rocks.

B **Combine each pair of sentences into a compound sentence. Use the coordinating conjunction or the semicolon and conjunctive adverb given. Add commas where needed.**

1. Many tourists visit Petra. They represent a danger to its conservation. (and)

   _____

2. The site of Petra is extensive. Its ruins spread over 400 square miles. (; in fact)

   _____

3. You have to walk a mile to enter the city. You can ride a horse or a horse-drawn cart. (or)

   _____

4. Petra's most famous monument is the Treasury. The building has an elaborate, carved facade. (and)

   _____

5. Petra's tombs and temples are magnificent. The pottery found there is of high artistic quality. (; in addition)

   _____

   _____

133 Exclamation Points and Question Marks

An **exclamation point** is used after an interjection or to end an exclamatory sentence.

> **Wow! You have a great bike.**
>
> **What a sleek-looking bike you have!**

A **question mark** is used to end an interrogative sentence.

> **Are you interested in bike racing?**

Add exclamation points and question marks where needed.
Also add periods as end marks where needed.

1. Do you know the story of Lance Armstrong

2. Incredible He won the Tour de France seven times

3. What is the Tour de France

4. Isn't it the most famous bicycle race in the world

5. What a grueling bicycle race it is

6. It usually lasts three weeks

7. Wow The riders even have to race up mountains

8. What do you know about racing bikes

9. I read that this type of bike is very lightweight, with a frame weighing only three pounds

10. Lance's feat is so impressive

11. Only one previous racer had won the race as many as five times

12. Did you know that Lance won all these races after he had treatments for cancer

13. He had to undergo chemotherapy and surgeries

14. He was determined, however, that he would race again

15. What a great athlete he is

16. Amazing Lance won the event for the first time in 1999, a few years after his treatments

17. Tremendous He formed a foundation to help cancer patients

18. Have you seen people wearing yellow wristbands to show their support for the foundation

19. Where can I find out more about this splendid athlete

20. Wait a minute I need more information on the next bike race

134 Semicolons and Colons

A **semicolon** is used

- to separate independent clauses in a compound sentence when the clauses are not joined by a conjunction

  Albert Schweitzer was first a musician and then a theologian; he eventually studied medicine also.

- to separate independent clauses in a compound sentence when the clauses are joined by a conjunctive adverb

  Albert Schweitzer first lived in France and Germany; however, he spent most of his life in Africa.

- to separate phrases or clauses of the same type that include internal punctuation

  Eventually he and his work received international recognition: honorary degrees; the Goethe Prize from Frankfurt, Germany; and the Nobel Peace Prize.

- before expressions such as *for example* and *namely* when they are used to introduce examples

  Schweitzer decided on his life's mission; namely, to serve the poor in Africa directly as a doctor.

A **colon** is used

- before a list of terms. A colon never follows a verb.

  Schweitzer excelled in the following areas: music, theology, and humanitarianism.

- after the salutation of a business letter

  Dear Sir or Madam:

Insert semicolons and colons where needed.

1. An act of heroism can last a moment for Albert Schweitzer it lasted a lifetime.

2. By age 28 Schweitzer had tried the following occupations pastor, musician, author, and professor.

3. He felt that his life was empty however, he eventually found his life's mission.

4. Schweitzer learned of the appalling problems in Africa poverty war and diseases such as malaria, leprosy, and sleeping sickness.

5. He decided what he would do namely, become a doctor and run a hospital in Africa.

6. His first year was full of the following activities gaining hospital experience, learning about Africa, and raising funds.

7. French Equatorial Africa became Schweitzer's home he set up a clinic in the city of Lambaréné.

8. His wife became his assistant she was a trained nurse.

9. The hospital became famous in fact, Schweitzer became known around the world.

10. In 1952 he was awarded a Nobel Peace Prize it was a fitting tribute to a man who had nobly served so many people who needed help.

135 Quotation Marks and Italics

Quotation marks are used

- to enclose dialogue and direct quotations. Single quotation marks set off a quotation within a quotation.

   "When," asked my father, "did an American soldier say, 'Lafayette, we are here'?"

- to set off the titles of stories, poems, songs, magazine articles, episodes of a TV series, and radio programs.

Italics are used for titles of books, movies, plays, newspapers, magazines, and works of art. In handwritten material, underlining is used to indicate italics.

A **Insert quotation marks and underlining where necessary.**

1. Be quiet! said Olive, I'm reading the Tribune.

2. Joseph's favorite poem is The Charge of the Light Brigade.

3. Thoreau wrote the book Walden and the essay Civil Disobedience.

4. I lost my copy of Great Expectations, Oswald said.

5. How long does 60 Minutes last? Jacob asked jokingly.

6. I thought it was fun, Al said, when we played 'Hail to the Chief.'

7. What time, asked Marge, does the movie My Fair Lady start?

8. The teacher asked, Have any of you read Lord of the Flies?

9. Have you ever heard of the Inner Sanctum radio program?

10. For his birthday Noam got a subscription to National Geographic.

B **Rewrite each sentence, adding punctuation where needed.**

1. The monkeys said Josephine are my favorite animals at the zoo

   _____

2. Twain wrote the novel Tom Sawyer and the short story The War Prayer

   _____

3. Look exclaimed Mr Donahue my picture is in the Chicago Tribune

   _____

4. Buzz Lightyear said Jane is my favorite character in Toy Story

   _____

5. The last time I saw him Harper told me he said I want to be a dancer

   _____

136 Apostrophes, Hyphens, and Dashes

An **apostrophe** is used

- to show possession: **Ed's car, the Caseys' house**
- to show the omission of letters or numbers: **isn't, '20s**
- to show the plural of lowercase letters but not capital letters unless the plural could be mistaken for a word: **r's, Rs, I's**

A **hyphen** is used

- to connect the parts of a compound number: **eighty-five, ninety-three**
- to separate the parts of some compound words: **run-through**
- to divide a word between syllables at the end of a line

A **dash** indicates a sudden change of thought.

The test—it covers three chapters—is next week.

A Insert apostrophes, hyphens, dashes, and other punctuation as needed.

1. Dont think that just anyone can run for the U S presidency
2. The president and the vice president must be at least thirty five years old
3. They must also be natural born citizens of the United States
4. The first seven presidents werent born U S citizens
5. They were born subjects of England the United States didnt exist yet
6. Presidents whove been elected to two terms are rare
7. Few presidents only seventeen out of forty four have done so
8. Franklin Roosevelt he was Teddy Roosevelts cousin was elected four times
9. But Roosevelts long tenure twelve years prompted new legislation
10. Now presidents may serve only two four year terms

B Rewrite the following sentences, adding apostrophes, hyphens, dashes, and other punctuation as needed.

1. Youre still going to Dr. Salks house, arent you

   _____

2. Herberts keyboard it doesnt have any is or us is broken

   _____

3. By midJanuary all of Jurgens relatives had gone back to Germany

   _____

4. Julias birthday she will be 38 years old is tomorrow

   _____

5. I didnt see the display of womens clothing

   _____

Punctuation & Capitalization

137 Capitalization

Use a **capital letter** for the following:

- the first word in a sentence
- the first word of a direct quotation
- the first word of most lines of poetry
- the titles of books, plays, poems, and works of art
- proper names and adjectives
- a title when it precedes a person's name

- the names of deities and the titles of sacred books
- the pronoun *I*
- *North, East, South,* and *West* when referring to sections of the country
- abbreviations when capital letters would be used if the words were written out

A Rewrite each item, capitalizing letters where necessary.

1. eva l. sloan, ph.d. _____
2. republican party _____
3. ohio river _____
4. private college _____
5. professor reiss _____
6. fourth of july _____
7. jesus christ _____
8. friday, may 3 _____
9. doctor _____
10. george w. bush _____

B Circle all letters that should be capitalized.

1. benjamin franklin was an american author, scientist, and statesman.
2. he helped draft the declaration of independence.
3. of this, he said, "we must all hang together, or assuredly we will all hang separately."
4. he was a member of the pennsylvania assembly for 12 years.
5. after the revolutionary war, franklin helped negotiate the treaty with england.
6. the treaty was signed at versailles, france, on september 3, 1783.
7. in 1732 he published *poor richard's almanac.*
8. in it he coined many phrases, such as "practice makes perfect."
9. he also wrote *the autobiography of benjamin franklin.*
10. as president of the pennsylvania abolition society, he urged the abolition of slavery.

138 Reviewing Punctuation & Capitalization

A **Insert commas, periods, question marks, and exclamation points where needed.**

1. Have you ever read *The War of the Worlds*

2. It is about Martians attacking Earth

3. How scary

4. It was written by H G Wells

5. He is well known for his stories of fantasy technology and science fiction

6. H G Wells also wrote *The Time Machine The Invisible Man* and *Ann Veronica*

7. *The War of the Worlds* was adapted and performed on the radio by Orson Welles in 1938

8. What happened

9. Many people believing the radio program was a news broadcast thought Earth was really being attacked

10. That's frightening

B **Insert colons, semicolons, and quotation marks where needed.**

11. Brooke's father told her to do the following mow, rake, and weed the lawn.

12. But I'm tired, she pleaded.

13. Her father said, Then you should not have stayed up all night.

14. She had rented some movies the night before therefore, she was up very late.

15. Brooke watched three movies *Casablanca, Gigi,* and *Ben-Hur.*

16. If you get started now, her father said, you can finish by nightfall.

17. She was exhausted nevertheless, she would do what he asked.

18. When I was a boy, her father said, we worked all day, or we didn't eat.

19. Here we go again, she thought to herself.

20. Brooke worked all afternoon she finished just before dark.

C **Insert hyphens, apostrophes, and dashes where needed.**

21. The fastest growing tree on earth is a member of the pea family.

22. One specimen grew thirty five feet in a year.

23. The tallest tree though not the largest is the sequoia.

24. Some old growth specimens are more than 300 feet high.

25. The worlds largest tree is the redwood.

26. A redwoods weight can be more than 200 tons.

27. Its not the oldest tree, however.

Continued →

Punctuation & Capitalization

138 Reviewing Punctuation & Capitalization, *continued*

28. One species of pine the worlds oldest tree can live 5,000 years.

29. These trees arent necessarily the oldest living things on earth.

30. Lichens plants made up of algae and fungus are also thousands of years old.

A Circle the example that is correctly capitalized in each row.

31. Harvard University	world war II	Mexican Silver
32. Mathematics	East Coast	Willis tower
33. Tuesday	Third avenue	asian
34. republicans	Lutherans	aunt Helga
35. *Of Mice And Men*	memorial day	spring in Paris
36. Nile river	sir Isaac Newton	October
37. Canadian border	Pacific ocean	Lakeview high school
38. Dictionary	middle East	Buddha
39. bible	Gettysburg address	The Time Machine
40. Frederick the great	Russian history	Dentist

Try It Yourself

On a separate sheet of paper, write six or seven sentences about what you will do after you have completed eighth grade. Be sure to punctuate your sentences carefully and correctly.

Check Your Own Work

Choose a selection from your writing portfolio, a journal, a work in progress, an assignment from another class, or a letter. Revise it, applying the skills you have reviewed. This checklist will help you.

✔ Do your sentences end with the correct punctuation?

✔ Have you used commas correctly?

✔ Have you used quotation marks before and after every quotation and around certain titles?

✔ Have you capitalized all proper nouns and adjectives?

✔ Have you used semicolons, colons, hyphens, and dashes where needed?

139 Simple Sentences

A **diagram** is a visual outline of a sentence. It shows the relationship between the words in a sentence.

- The subject, the verb, the direct object, the subject complement, and the object complement go on the main horizontal line.
- A vertical line that cuts through the main line separates the subject from the verb, and a vertical line that does not cut through the main line separates the direct object from the verb.
- A line that slants to the left separates a subject complement from the verb, and a line that slants to the right separates an object complement from the direct object.
- Indirect objects, adjectives, and adverbs are placed under the words to which they relate. Prepositional phrases, which usually act as adjectives or adverbs, go under the words they describe.

SENTENCE: **Richard gave Will advice.**

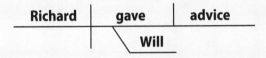

SENTENCE: **The cookies are chewy.**

SENTENCE: **We elected Elaine secretary.**

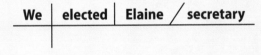

SENTENCE: **The sleek horse ran swiftly.**

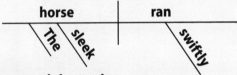

SENTENCE: **The horse with the shiny black coat ran around the track.**

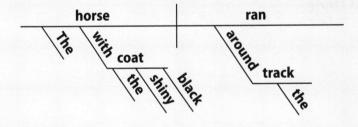

Diagram each sentence.

1. My favorite subject is science.

2. Sugar gives your body quick energy.

© Loyola Press. Exercises in English   **Level H**

Diagramming

Continued → 151

3. They named their dog Jake.

4. The movers pushed the heavy piano up the ramp.

5. A veranda is a big porch with a roof.

6. The sky was dark before the storm.

7. Peter's aunt sent him a red homemade scarf.

140 Appositives

- An appositive is placed in parentheses to the right of the word it identifies.
- Words that describe the appositive go under it.

SENTENCE: I read *A Christmas Carol,* a famous book by Charles Dickens.

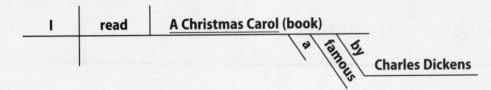

Diagram each sentence.

1. My sister is taking a class in botany, the study of plants.

2. James Cook, a British sailor, explored the Pacific in the 1760s.

3. My brother Roberto is studying Chinese.

4. Ramadan, a month in the Muslim calendar, is a time of fasting.

Continued → 153

5. Chicle, juice from a tropical tree, is the main ingredient in chewing gum.

6. Many tourists ride the London Eye, a big Ferris wheel.

7. The dog Snoopy was created by Charles M. Schulz , a cartoonist.

8. The poet James Berry writes about his Caribbean homeland.

9. The writer Henry Wadsworth Longfellow wrote the poem "Paul Revere's Ride."

10. Abolitionism, a movement against slavery, gained a number of supporters in the early 1800s.

141 Compound Sentences

- Each independent clause of a compound sentence has its own horizontal line, with its subject, verb, objects, and complements in their usual positions.
- The coordinating conjunction or conjunctive adverb that connects the clauses is placed on a vertical dashed line that touches the left edges of the main horizontal lines.

SENTENCE: I bought a blank book, and I used it for a diary.

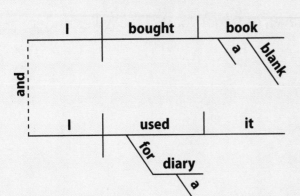

SENTENCE: The novel was short; consequently, I finished it in one day.

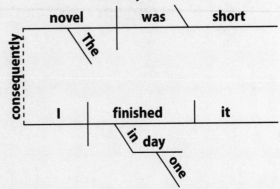

Diagram each sentence.

1. Sharks have a good sense of smell, but their eyesight is poor.

2. Sally Ride was the first American female astronaut; therefore, many people admire her.

Continued →

3. The campers sat around the fire, and they told scary stories.

4. An iceberg can appear very big; however, its largest part actually lies under the water.

5. South Dakota was part of the Louisiana Purchase, and it became a state in 1889.

6. Waves hit the beach, and seagulls flew overhead.

7. I can read my book, or I can watch TV.

Diagramming

142 Compound Sentence Elements

- Compound subjects and compound predicates are placed on two separate horizontal lines that are joined to the main horizontal line.
- The conjunction connecting the compound parts is placed on a vertical line between them.
- Each subject may have its own modifiers, and each verb may have its own objects, complements, and modifiers.
- Words other than subjects and verbs may also be compound. They are diagrammed in a similar way.

SENTENCE: Allison and I saw the concert and got autographs from a band member.

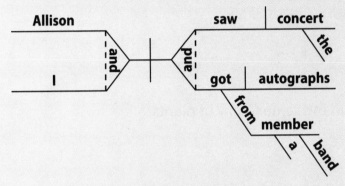

SENTENCE: Her stories are always funny and creative.

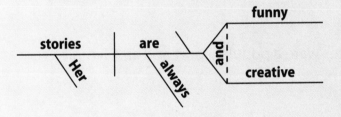

Diagram each sentence.

1. My collage contains beans and beads.

2. Similes and metaphors are figures of speech.

Continued → **157**

3. The water froze and solidified.

4. The ship entered the harbor and docked at a pier.

5. Lettuce and sunflowers are in the same family of plants.

6. In ancient Greece, chariot races were a popular sport and an Olympic event.

7. German shepherds are famous for their intelligence and loyalty.

8. I dug holes in the ground and planted the pumpkin seeds.

143 Participles

- The participle in a participial phrase starts on a slanted line under the noun or pronoun it describes and extends onto a horizontal line.
- Any direct object or complement is placed on the horizontal line after the participle.
- Modifiers of the participle, its object, or its complement go on slanted lines under the word being described.
- A participle that precedes the noun it describes is positioned as other adjectives are.

SENTENCE: Cleaning the closet, I found my old skates.

SENTENCE: An unopened letter lay on the desk.

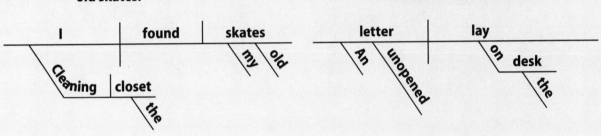

Diagram each sentence.

1. In 1872 President Grant signed a bill creating Yellowstone Park.

2. Jumping into the water, Moira splashed the people sitting near the pool.

3. The Northern Lights have a shimmering beauty.

Continued →

4. Walking down the beach, the child gathered seashells.

5. Spanish galleons carrying gold from the Americas crossed the Atlantic in the 1500s.

6. The doctor knelt over the injured boy.

7. Fran gazed at the pictures hanging on the walls.

8. Congress must not make laws prohibiting freedom of speech.

© Loyola Press. Exercises in English   Level H

144 Gerunds

- A gerund is placed according to its function in a sentence—as a subject, a subject complement, an object of a verb, an object of a preposition, or an appositive.
- The gerund is placed on a stepped line that rests on a stem connected to the horizontal line.
- A direct object or a complement is placed after the gerund. Modifiers are placed as usual.
- When used as the object of a preposition, a gerund goes on a stepped line but is not raised.

SENTENCE: **Making supper on Friday evening is my job.**   SENTENCE: **Looms are used for weaving cloth.**

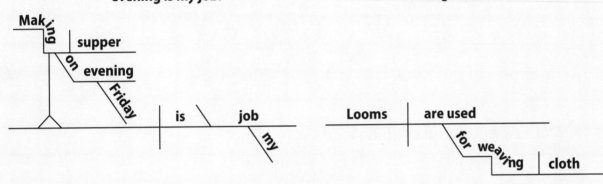

Diagram each sentence.

1. Having friends is important.

2. The plants need watering.

3. Writing a poem is making music.

Diagramming

Continued → 161

4. My mother's hobby, singing in the choir, requires weekly rehearsals.

5. We started gathering seashells on the beach.

6. Molars are useful for crushing food.

7. An important industry in Australia is raising sheep.

8. The idea of protecting land for wildlife originated in the 1800s.

9. We started doing research for our science project.

145 Infinitives

- An infinitive is placed according to its function in a sentence—as a noun, an adjective, or an adverb. When used as a subject, a direct object, a subject complement, or an appositive, an infinitive is placed in the appropriate position over a stem above the main line.

- As in a prepositional phrase, the word *to* is placed on a slanted line; the verb is on a horizontal line.

- A direct object or a complement of the infinitive follows the verb on the horizontal line. Modifiers are placed in their usual positions.

- When used as an adjective or an adverb, an infinitive is placed under the word it describes.

SENTENCE: **We decided to order pizza for supper.**

SENTENCE: **I was surprised to get a big package in the mail.**

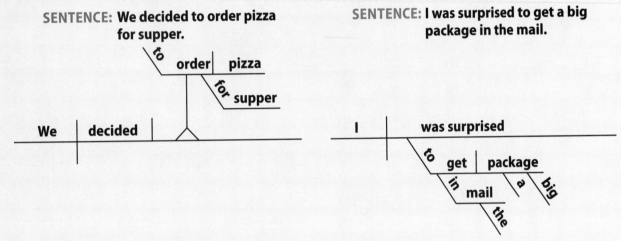

Diagram each sentence.

1. To speak Spanish well is my goal.

2. Jackson is saving to buy a new bicycle.

3. Chess seems difficult to play.

Diagramming

Continued →

4. People first began to keep records on clay tablets.

5. The best place to see the Northern Lights is located in the northern part of Alaska.

6. My brother wants to learn skiing.

7. My suggestion, to organize a bake sale, was accepted.

8. To consider bills for passage is Congress's job.

9. The park is a good place to have a picnic.

146 Adjective Clauses

- An adjective clause is placed on a horizontal line parallel to and under the horizontal line of the independent clause.
- A dashed line connects the relative pronoun or the subordinate conjunction in the adjective clause to the word in the independent clause that the clause describes. *Whose,* like other possessives, goes under the noun it is associated with.
- A relative pronoun is placed according to its function within the adjective clause.

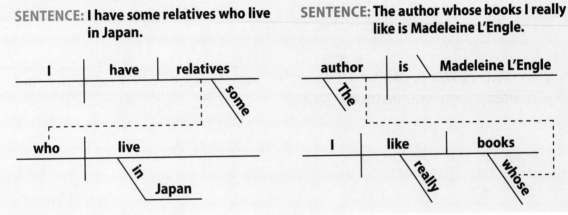

SENTENCE: **I have some relatives who live in Japan.**

SENTENCE: **The author whose books I really like is Madeleine L'Engle.**

Diagram each sentence.

1. Silkworms, which are really caterpillars, feed on mulberry leaves.

2. Lightning is electricity that people can see.

3. The Newbery Medal, which is awarded yearly, honors the best children's book.

4. In the attic my mother found some antiques that belonged to my grandmother.

5. The Aztecs, whose capital occupied the site of present-day Mexico City, had created a large empire by the 1400s.

6. People who are good swimmers generally enjoy sailing also.

7. My brother got the job that he wanted.

147 Adverb Clauses

- An adverb clause goes on a horizontal line under the independent clause.
- The subordinate conjunction is placed on a slanting dashed line that connects the verb in the adverb clause with the word in the independent clause that the adverb clause describes, which is usually the verb.

SENTENCE: After I learn Spanish, I want to visit Spain.

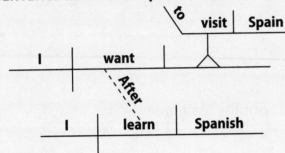

Diagram each sentence.

1. If you follow the directions carefully, you can easily make bread.

2. Few outsiders visited the Himalayas until the airplane was invented.

3. Although most grasshoppers can fly, they usually move by jumping.

Diagramming

Continued → **167**

4. After several Southern states left the Union at the time of the Civil War, they formed the Confederacy.

5. I started doing research as soon as I got the assignment.

6. When light passes through a prism, it becomes a band of many colors.

7. Dandelions spread rapidly because they do not need pollination.

Name .... Date ....

148 Noun Clauses

- A noun clause is placed according to its function in the sentence. It has its own horizontal line that rests on a stem connecting it to the horizontal line of the independent clause.

- Noun clauses, with the exception of those used as objects of prepositions, are placed above the main clause.

- If the word introducing the noun clause has a specific function in the noun clause, it is placed according to that function. If it has no specific function, it is placed on the vertical line that connects the noun clause to the independent clause.

SENTENCE: **I decided that I need a new bike.**

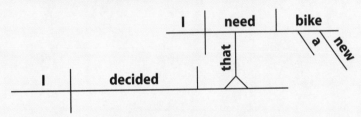

SENTENCE: **The teacher promised extra points to whoever could name all of the presidents.**

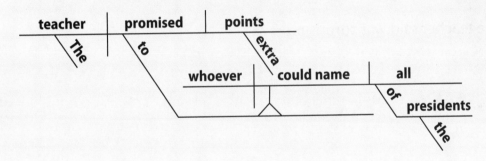

Diagram each sentence.

1. Some people believe that the Northern Lights are spirits in the sky.

2. I could not believe what my friend told me.

© Loyola Press. Exercises in English   **Level H**

Diagramming

Continued →

3. With an experiment in 1804, Thomas Young showed that light is waves.

4. That Shakespeare was the greatest writer in English is an opinion held by many.

5. What the teacher said was surprising.

6. That laughter is a good medicine is a common belief.

7. The idea that the nation should remain united motivated Abraham Lincoln.

© Loyola Press. Exercises in English **Level H**

Diagramming

149 Diagramming Review

- Subjects, verbs, direct objects, and complements go on the main horizontal line. Adjectives, adverbs, prepositional phrases, and participles go under the words they describe.

- Gerunds and infinitives may go above or below the main line depending on how they are used in a sentence.

- Compound sentences and sentences with adjective clauses, adverb clauses, and noun clauses have two horizontal lines connected by dashed lines. An adjective clause or an adverb clause is placed on its own horizontal line under the line for the main clause. The line for a noun clause may go above the main horizontal line.

SENTENCE: Having eaten my entire lunch at ten, I was very hungry again by noon.

SENTENCE: Our plan is to travel west by car.

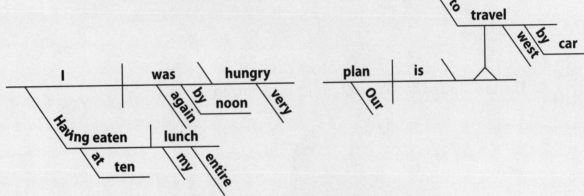

SENTENCE: Sarah arranged the flowers that she picked from the garden.

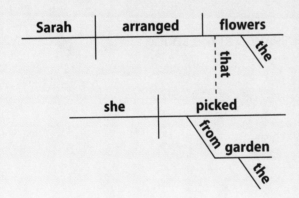

Diagram each sentence.

1. Solving crossword puzzles is fun.

Diagramming

Continued →

2. Paula described what she did on her trip.

3. When we eat peas and corn, we are eating seeds.

4. The law states that a person must be a citizen to vote.

5. Cotton plants are annuals and are planted in the spring.

6. The theaters of the ancient Greeks were built in the open air and were made of stone.

Handbook of Terms

ADJECTIVES

An **adjective** points out or describes a noun.

An **article** points out a noun. *A, an,* and *the* are articles: *a* game, *an* apple, *the* rules.

A **demonstrative adjective** points out a specific person, place, or thing. *This, that, these,* and *those* are demonstrative adjectives: *this* book, *those* pencils.

A **descriptive adjective** tells about the age, size, shape, color, origin, or another quality of a noun. A descriptive adjective usually comes before the noun it describes, but it may follow the noun. It may also follow a linking verb: It was a *sunny* morning. The popcorn, *crunchy* and *salty,* tasted *great.*

An **indefinite adjective** refers to any or all members of a group. Indefinite adjectives include *all, another, any, both, each, either, few, many, more, most, much, neither, other, several,* and *some*: *both* boys, *either* girl.

An **interrogative adjective** is used in questions. *What, which,* and *whose* are interrogative adjectives: *Whose* book is this?

A **possessive adjective** shows possession or ownership. The possessive adjectives are *my, your, his, her, its, our, your,* and *their*: *my* car, *your* motorcycle.

A **proper adjective** is formed from a proper noun. A proper adjective begins with a capital letter: *American* history.

See also **Antecedents, Clauses, Comparisons, Participles, Prepositions, Sentences, Subject-Verb Agreement.**

ADVERBS

An **adverb** modifies a verb, an adjective, or another adverb. Many adverbs end with *ly*.

- An **adverb of affirmation** tells that something is positive or gives consent or approval: The music is *certainly* beautiful.
- An **adverb of degree** answers the question *how much* or *how little*: The boy is *very* tall.
- An **adverb of manner** answers the question *how* or *in what manner*: Jason draws *well*.
- An **adverb of negation** expresses a negative condition or refusal: The door is *not* locked.
- An **adverb of place** answers the question *where*: Sit *here* by the gate.
- An **adverb of time** answers the question *when* or *how often*: It rained *yesterday*.

An **adverbial noun** is a noun that functions as an adverb. An adverbial noun expresses time, measure, value, or direction: Every *Sunday* we attend church. He ran six *miles*.

A **conjunctive adverb** is used to connect two independent clauses. The principal conjunctive adverbs are *consequently, however, moreover, nevertheless, therefore,* and *thus*: Jill had studied journalism; *therefore*, the newspaper editor hired her.

An **interrogative adverb** is used in asking questions. *Why, where, when,* and *how* are interrogative adverbs: *When* did you do that?

See also **Clauses, Comparisons, Prepositions.**

ANTECEDENTS

The noun to which a pronoun or a possessive adjective refers is its **antecedent.** A pronoun or a possessive adjective must agree with its antecedent in person and number. A third person singular pronoun or possessive adjective must also agree with its antecedent in gender.

See also **Adjectives, Pronouns.**

CAPITALIZATION

Capital letters are used for many purposes, including the following:

- The first word of a sentence: The bell rang.
- Proper nouns and proper adjectives: Betsy Ross, American flag
- An abbreviation if the word it stands for begins with a capital letter: Rev. for Reverend
- The first word and the name of a person addressed in the salutation of a letter and the first word in the close of a letter: Dear Marie, Yours truly
- The principal words in the titles of books, plays, works of art, and poems: *A Tale of Two Cities, Romeo and Juliet, Mona Lisa,* "Fire and Ice"
- The first word of a direct quotation: Mother said, "It's time for my favorite television program."
- Titles when used in direct address as a substitute for the person's name: Thank you, Professor.
- *North, East, South, West* when they refer to sections of the country or the world. They are not capitalized when they refer to directions: the Old West. He drove west on Main Street.
- The pronoun *I*
- Names referring to deities or to sacred books: God, the Bible
- Two-letter state postal abbreviations: MA, NY, CA

Handbook of Terms

174

© Loyola Press. Exercises in English **Level H**

CLAUSES

A **clause** is a group of related words that contains a subject and predicate.

A **dependent clause** does not express a complete thought and cannot stand alone. A dependent clause, together with an independent clause, forms a complex sentence.

- An **adjective clause** is a dependent clause used as an adjective. An adjective clause is usually introduced by a relative pronoun, such as *who, whom, which, whose,* or *that*: The roses *that he bought* were yellow.

- An **adverb clause** is a dependent clause used as an adverb. An adverb clause is usually introduced by a subordinate conjunction such as *after, although, as, because, before, for, since, that, though, unless, until, when, where,* or *while*: *After we had canoed down the river,* we went to a clambake on the beach.

- A **noun clause** is a dependent clause used as a noun. Most noun clauses begin with an introductory word such as *that, who, whom, whoever, whomever, how, why, when, whether, what, where,* or *whatever*: *That he was late* disappointed me.

An **independent clause** expresses a complete thought. An independent clause can stand alone as a sentence.

A **nonrestrictive clause** is a dependent clause that adds information about a person, place, or thing, but it is not necessary to the meaning of the sentence. A nonrestrictive clause is separated from the rest of the sentence by commas: New York City, *which is located on the eastern seaboard,* contains many skyscrapers.

A **restrictive clause** is a dependent clause that points out or identifies a certain person, place, or thing. A restrictive clause cannot be omitted without changing the meaning of a sentence: The girl *who runs fastest* will win the prize.

See also **Sentences.**

COMPARISONS

Many adjectives and adverbs can be used to compare two or more people, places, things, or actions.

- The **positive degree** describes one or more people, places, things, or actions: The *tall* boy ran *fast*.

- The **comparative degree** compares two people, places, things, or actions. Form comparatives by adding *-er* to the positive degree or by putting *more* or *less* before the positive degree: The *younger* child cried *more sadly*.

- The **superlative degree** compares three or more people, places, things, or actions. Form superlatives by adding *-est* to the positive degree or by putting *most* or *least* before the positive degree: The *tallest* boy ran *most quickly*.

Few, fewer, and *fewest* are used to compare count nouns. *Little, less,* and *least* are used to compare noncount nouns: *few* dimes, *little* money.

Handbook of Terms

Farther and *further* are used both as adverbs and as adjectives. *Farther* refers to distance; *further* denotes an addition: She went *farther* into the forest. *Further* research is necessary.

Comparisons with *as . . . as* may be made in positive or negative sentences. Comparisons with *so . . . as* may be made only in negative sentences. *As* is never used with *equally* in a comparison: Bill is *as* tall *as* Kelly. John cannot run *so* fast *as* Mike.

The conjunctions *than* and *as* are used to join clauses to make comparisons. Often part of the second clause is omitted. The omitted part must be added mentally to determine whether the pronoun needed is a subject pronoun or an object pronoun: Gary was *as* surprised *as she* (was surprised). Laura gave Tom more candy *than* (she gave) *me*.

CONJUNCTIONS

A conjunction is used to connect words, phrases, or clauses in a sentence.

A **coordinating conjunction** connects words, phrases, or clauses of the same rank and function. *And, or, but, so, nor,* and *yet* are coordinating conjunctions: Todd *or* Cindy will come early to help us.

Correlative conjunctions are conjunctions used in pairs: *Neither* Tom *nor* Laurie came to the party.

A **conjunctive adverb** connects two independent clauses. It is preceded by a semicolon and followed by a comma: The meal was expensive; *however,* I wasn't surprised.

A **subordinate conjunction** introduces a dependent clause and connects it to an independent clause: He missed gym class *because* he was sick.

See also **Adverbs, Clauses, Sentences.**

GERUNDS

A **gerund** is a verb form ending in *-ing* that is used as a noun. A **gerund phrase** is a gerund along with any direct object, complement, and/or modifiers. A gerund or a gerund phrase can be used as a subject, a subject complement, a direct object, an object of a preposition, or an appositive: *Swimming* is good exercise. She enjoys *cooking elaborate meals*.

A gerund may be preceded by a possessive noun or a possessive adjective. The possessive describes the doer of the action of the gerund: *My* arriving early was a surprise.

INFINITIVES

An **infinitive** is a verb form, usually preceded by *to,* that can be used as a noun, an adjective, or an adverb. An **infinitive phrase** is an infinitive and its direct object, complement, and/or modifiers. An infinitive or an infinitive phrase used as a noun can be a subject, a subject complement, a direct object, an object of a preposition, or an appositive: *To win* was our goal. He wanted *to earn some money*.

Handbook of Terms

A **hidden infinitive,** one in which the word *to* is not used, appears after verbs such as *hear, see, know, feel, let, make,* and *help* and with the prepositions *but* and *except* and the conjunction *than:* I helped her *construct* the framework.

A **split infinitive** results when an adverb is placed between *to* and the verb. Split infinitives generally should be avoided.

INTERJECTIONS

An **interjection** expresses a strong or sudden emotion, such as delight, disgust, pain, agreement, impatience, surprise, sorrow, or wonder. An interjection is grammatically distinct from the rest of the sentence: *Oh! Shh! Ouch! Wow!*

MOOD

Mood shows the manner in which the action or state of being of a verb is expressed.

- The **imperative mood** is used to give commands: Please *call* me.
- The **indicative mood** is used to state a fact or ask a question: Where *are* you?
- The **subjunctive mood** is used to express a wish or a desire or a condition that is contrary to fact. The subjunctive is also used to express a demand or a recommendation after *that*: She wishes she *were coming* with us. If she *had* more money, she would come. Her mother recommended that she *get* a job.

NOUNS

A **noun** is the name of a person, place, or thing. A noun can be used as the subject, an appositive, the direct object, the indirect object, the object of a preposition, or the subject complement in a sentence.

A **collective noun** names a group of people, places, or things considered as a unit. A collective noun usually takes a verb that agrees with a singular noun: The *crew* is tired. The *herd* is resting.

A **common noun** names any one member of a group of people, places, or things: *queen, city, church.*

A **concrete noun** names a thing that can be seen or touched: *brother, river, tree.*

An **abstract noun** names something that cannot be seen or touched: respect, fear, bravery.

A **plural noun** names more than one person, place, or thing: *boys, berries, geese.*

A **possessive noun** expresses possession or ownership.

- To form the possessive of a singular noun, add -'s to the singular form: *architect's*.
- To form the possessive of a plural noun that ends in *s*, add an apostrophe to the plural form: *farmers'*.
- To form the possessive of a plural noun that does not end in *s*, add -'s to the plural form: *children's*.
- To show separate possession, add -'s to each noun: *Meg's* and *Mike's* dogs.
- To show joint possession, add -'s to the last noun only: *Jack* and *Jill's* pail.

A **proper noun** names a particular person, place, or thing. A proper noun is capitalized: *Queen Elizabeth, London, Westminster Abbey*.

A **singular noun** names one person, place, or thing: *boy, river, berry*.

See also **Clauses, Gerunds, Infinitives, Prepositions, Sentences, Subject-Verb Agreement.**

PARTICIPLES

A **participle** is a verb form that can be used as an adjective. Present participles end in *-ing,* and past participles often end in *-ed.* A participle used as an adjective can come before or after the noun it modifies or after a linking verb: The *broiled* chicken tasted great. The cake *baking* in the oven smelled delicious. The lemonade was *refreshing*.

A participial adjective that does not modify any noun or pronoun in a sentence is called a **dangling participle.** Sentences with dangling participles must be rewritten.

PREPOSITIONS

A **preposition** is a word that shows the relationship between a noun or a pronoun and some other word in the sentence. The **object of a preposition** is the noun or pronoun that follows the preposition: The huge mountain lion leaped *through* (preposition) the tall *grass* (object of the preposition).

A **prepositional phrase** is a phrase that is introduced by a preposition.

- An **adjective phrase** is used as an adjective and modifies a noun or a pronoun: The cabin *in the woods* burned down.
- An **adverb phrase** is used as an adverb and usually modifies a verb: The river flows *into the sea*.
- A **noun phrase** is used as a noun. It can be used as a subject or a subject complement: *Before dinner* is a good time to do your homework.

PRONOUNS

A **pronoun** is a word that takes the place of a noun or nouns.

A **demonstrative pronoun** points out a definite person, place, or thing. *This, that, these,* and *those* are demonstrative pronouns: *This* is mine. *Those* are yours.

An **indefinite pronoun** refers to any or all of a group of people, places, or things. Among the indefinite pronouns are *all, another, both, each, either, few, many, neither, nothing, several, some,* and pronouns beginning with *any* or *every*: *Each* wants to be on the team. *Both* must pass physicals.

An **intensive pronoun** is used to show emphasis. The intensive pronouns are *myself, yourself, himself, herself, itself, ourselves, yourselves,* and *themselves*: I *myself* cooked the entire dinner.

An **interrogative pronoun** is used to ask a question. The interrogative pronouns are *who, whom, which, what,* and *whose*: To *whom* does this belong?

An **object pronoun** is used as the direct or indirect object of a verb or as the object of a preposition. The object pronouns are *me, you, him, her, it, us,* and *them.*

Personal pronouns have different forms.

- A personal pronoun shows **person**: the speaker **(first person),** the person spoken to **(second person),** or the person, place, or thing spoken about **(third person).** The first person pronouns are *I, me, mine, we, us,* and *ours.* The second person pronouns are *you* and *yours.* The third person pronouns are *he, him, his, she, her, hers, it, its, they, them,* and *theirs.*

- A personal pronoun shows **number.** It is **singular** when it refers to one person, place, or thing. The singular pronouns are *I, me, mine, you, yours, he, him, his, she, her, hers, it,* and *its.* A personal pronoun is **plural** when it refers to more than one person, place, or thing. The plural pronouns are *we, us, ours, you, yours, they, their,* and *theirs.*

- The third person singular pronoun shows **gender.** It can be **masculine** *(he, him, his),* **feminine** *(she, her, hers),* or **neuter** *(it, its).*

A **possessive pronoun** shows possession or ownership. The possessive pronouns are *mine, yours, his, hers, its, ours,* and *theirs.* A possessive pronoun takes the place of a noun and its possessive adjective. Although possessive pronouns show ownership, they do not contain apostrophes: The new skates are *hers.*

A **reflexive pronoun** can be used as a direct or an indirect object or as the object of a preposition. The reflexive pronouns are *myself, yourself, himself, herself, itself, ourselves, yourselves,* and *themselves*: She made *herself* a sandwich.

A **relative pronoun** connects a noun clause to the person, place, or thing it modifies. The relative pronouns are *who, whom, whose, which,* and *that*: Hal, *who* grew up in Indonesia, now lives in Boston.

A **subject pronoun** is used as a subject or a subject complement. The subject pronouns are *I, you, he, she, it, we,* and *they*: *We* played soccer. The goalie was *he.*

See also **Antecedents, Clauses, Comparisons, Gerunds, Sentences, Subject-Verb Agreement.**

Handbook of Terms

PUNCTUATION

An **apostrophe** (') is used as follows:

- To show ownership: the *cook's* hat, the *girls'* horses
- To replace letters or numbers that are omitted: *wasn't, '76*
- With *s* to show the plural of lowercase letters but not capital letters unless the plural could be mistaken for a word: *p*'s and *q*'s, *R*s and *A*'s

A **colon** (:) is used as follows:

- After the salutation in a business letter: Dear Sir:
- Before a list when terms such as *follows* or *the following* are used: We bought the following: eggs, limes, bread.

A **comma** (,) is used to make reading clearer. Among the comma's uses are the following:

- To separate words or groups of words in a series and adjectives of equal importance before nouns: On a hot, sunny day we saw elephants, giraffes, hyenas, and monkeys.
- To set off parts of dates, addresses, or geographical names: January 1, 2003; 321 Spring Road, Atlanta, Georgia
- To set off a word in direct address: Josie, I'm so pleased that you called me this morning.
- After the word *yes* or *no* when it introduces a sentence: Yes, I agree with you completely.
- To set off a direct quotation, unless a question mark or exclamation point is required: "We have only vanilla and chocolate today," he said in an apologetic tone.
- Before a coordinating conjunction or after a conjunctive adverb in a compound sentence: She called his name, but he didn't answer her. She became angry; however, she soon got over it.
- After the salutation of a friendly letter and after the closing of a letter: Dear Ben, Sincerely yours,
- To set off a parenthetical expression—a word or a group of words that is inserted into a sentence as a comment or explanatory remark but is not necessary to the meaning of the sentence: The time, I think, is up.
- After a long introductory phrase or after an introductory clause: As the band marched down the street, the class cheered and applauded.
- To separate nonrestrictive phrases and clauses from the rest of the sentence: Chicago, which is the largest city in Illinois, is not the state capital.

A **dash** (—) is used to indicate a sudden change of thought: The boy jumped—indeed soared—over the hurdle.

An **exclamation point** (!) is used after an interjection and after an exclamatory sentence: Wow! What a celebration that was!

A **hyphen** (-) is used as follows:

- To divide a word at the end of a line whenever one or more syllables are carried to the next line.
- In the words for numbers from twenty-one to ninety-nine and between the parts of some compound words: *soldier-statesman, half-baked* plan.

A **period** (.) is used at the end of a declarative or an imperative sentence and after initials and some abbreviations: Pres. J. F. Kennedy was from Massachusetts.

A **question mark** (?) is used at the end of an interrogative sentence: What time is it?

Quotation marks (". . .") are used as follows:

- Before and after every direct quotation and every part of a divided quotation: "Let's go shopping," said Michiko. "I can go with you," Father said, "after I have eaten lunch."
- To enclose titles of short stories, poems, and magazine articles. Titles of books, magazines, newspapers, movies, TV shows, and works of art are usually printed in italics or are underlined: I read "The Lost City" in *Newsweek*.

A **semicolon** (;) is used as follows:

- To separate the clauses of a compound sentence when they are not separated by a conjunction: I can't ride my bike; the wheel is damaged.
- To separate the clauses of a compound sentence that are connected by a conjunctive adverb: Helga plays the violin; however, she can barely read music.
- To separate phrases or clauses that have internal punctuation: We went to Paris, France; Rome, Italy; and London, England.
- Before expressions such as *for example* or *namely* when they are used to introduce examples: He achieved his goals; namely, acceptance into college and a scholarship.

SENTENCES

A sentence is a group of words that expresses a complete thought. A sentence must have a subject and a predicate and may contain other elements.

- An **appositive** is a word or group of words that follows a noun or a pronoun in a sentence and renames it: Kanisha Taylor, the *president* of our class, will make the first speech.
- A **direct object** is the receiver of the action of a verb. A noun or an object pronoun can be used as a direct object: Nat helped *him* with his homework.
- An **indirect object** is a noun or an object pronoun that tells *to whom, to what, for whom,* or *for what* the action in a sentence is done: I gave *him* a present.
- A **predicate** tells something about the subject. The **simple predicate** is a verb or verb phrase: Teresa *waved*. The **complete predicate** is the verb with all its modifiers, objects, and complements: Teresa *waved to the child from the window*.
- An **object complement** follows a direct object and completes the thought expressed by the verb. An object complement can be a noun or an adjective: They elected Jim *president*. He found the job *difficult*.
- A **subject** names the person, place, or thing a sentence is about. The **simple subject** is a noun or a pronoun: The *man* is riding his bike. The **complete subject** is the simple subject with all its modifiers: *The tall, athletic, young man* is riding his bike.
- A **subject complement** is a word that completes the meaning of a sentence that has a linking verb. A subject complement may be a noun, a pronoun, or an adjective: Broccoli is a green *vegetable*. The winner was *she*. The sea will be *cold*.

A **complex sentence** contains one independent clause and one or more dependent clauses: *If you want to win, you must jump higher.*

- A **dependent clause** does not express a complete thought and cannot stand alone: *If you want to win*

- An **independent clause** expresses a complete thought: *You must jump higher.*

A **compound sentence** contains two or more independent clauses.

- The clauses in a compound sentence are usually connected by a conjunction or by a conjunctive adverb: Usually Jane drives to work, *but* today she took the train. She left early; *nevertheless,* she was late for work.

- A semicolon may be used to separate the clauses in a compound sentence: She left on time; the train was late.

A **declarative sentence** makes a statement. A declarative sentence is followed by a period: The sun is shining.

An **exclamatory sentence** expresses strong or sudden emotion. An exclamatory sentence is followed by an exclamation point: What a loud noise that was!

An **imperative sentence** gives a command or makes a request. An imperative sentence is followed by a period: Go to the store. Please pick up the papers.

An **interrogative sentence** asks a question. An interrogative sentence is followed by a question mark: Where is my pen?

A **simple sentence** contains one subject and one predicate. Either or both may be compound. Any objects and/or complements may also be compound: *Ivan* and *John* argued with the grocer. The baby *walks* and *talks* well. Wear your *hat, scarf,* and *gloves.*

See also **Clauses, Subject-Verb Agreement.**

SUBJECT-VERB AGREEMENT

A subject and a verb must always agree.

- A phrase or a parenthetical expression between the subject and the verb does not affect the verb: A *crate* of bananas *was* hoisted off the boat.

- Indefinite pronouns such as *anyone, anything, everybody, no one, nobody, nothing, one, somebody,* and *something* and indefinite adjectives such as *another, each, either, neither,* and *other* always require the verb that agrees with the third person singular. Possessive adjectives and pronouns that refer to these words must be singular: *Everyone* in this class *works* hard for *his* or *her* grades. *Neither* girl *was doing her* homework on the bus.

- Indefinite pronouns such as *both, few,* and *many* and indefinite adjectives such as *all, any, most,* and *some* generally require the verb that agrees with the third person plural. Possessive adjectives and pronouns that refer to these words must be plural: *Few look* to *their* left before turning. *Most* puppies *enjoy their* treats.

- A collective noun is singular if the idea expressed by the subject is thought of as a unit: The orchestra *plays* tomorrow. A collective noun is plural if the idea expressed by the subject is thought of as individuals: The family *are* living in Georgia, Virginia, and the Carolinas.
- In sentences beginning with *there,* use *there is* or *there was* when the subject that follows is singular. Use *there are* or *there were* when the subject is plural: *There is* no cause for alarm. *There were* many passengers on the bus.
- Compound subjects connected by *and* are generally plural. If, however, the subjects connected by *and* refer to the same person, place, or thing or express a single idea, the subject is considered singular: Bob and Ted *are* making breakfast. Ham and eggs *is* their favorite meal.
- When compound subjects are connected by *or* or *nor,* the verb agrees with the subject closer to it: *Neither* Ken *nor* the twins *are* here. *Neither* the twins *nor* Ken *is* here.
- When two or more subjects connected by *and* are preceded by *each, every, many a,* or *no,* the subject is considered singular: *Every* teacher and student *has heard* the news.

TENSES

The tense of a verb shows the time of its action.

- The **simple present tense** tells about something that is always true or about an action that happens again and again: I *play* the piano every afternoon.
- The **simple past tense** tells about an action that happened in the past: I *played* the piano yesterday afternoon.
- The **future tense** tells about an action that will happen in the future. The future is formed with the present and the auxiliary verb *will* or the verb phrase *going to* with a form of the verb *be*: The piano recital *will be* on Sunday. I *am going to play* two songs.
- The **present progressive tense** tells what is happening now. The present progressive tense is formed with the present participle and a form of the verb *be*: He *is eating* his lunch now.
- The **past progressive tense** tells what was happening in the past. The past progressive tense is formed with the present participle and a past form of the verb *be*: He *was eating* his lunch when I saw him.
- The **present perfect tense** tells about a past action that is relevant to the present. The present perfect tense is formed with *have* or *has* and the past participle: I *have lived* here for six years now.
- The **past perfect tense** tells about a past action that happened before another past action. The past perfect tense is formed with *had* and the past participle: I *had lived* in Memphis for a year before I moved here.
- The **future perfect tense** tells about an action that will be completed by a specific time in the future. The future perfect tense is formed with *will have* and the past participle: I *will have finished* dinner by the time you get here.

VERBALS

A **verbal** is a verb form used as a noun, an adjective, or an adverb. *See* **Gerunds, Infinitives, Participles.**

VERBS

A **verb** is a word that expresses action or state of being.

An **intransitive verb** has no receiver of the action. It does not have a direct object: The sun *shone* on the lake.

A **linking verb** links a subject with a subject complement (a noun, a pronoun, or an adjective).

- The verb *be* in its many forms (*is, are, was, will be, have been,* etc.) is the most common linking verb: He *is* happy. They *are* students.
- The verbs *appear, become, continue, feel, grow, look, remain, seem, smell, sound,* and *taste* are also considered linking verbs: This *tastes* good. She *became* president.

Modal auxiliary verbs such as *may, might, can, could, must, should,* and *would* are used to express permission, possibility, ability, necessity, and obligation: You *should* hurry. We *might be* late.

A verb has four **principal parts**: the present, the present participle, the past, and the past participle.

- The present participle is formed by adding *-ing* to the present: *walking, running.*
- The simple past and the past participle of **regular verbs** are formed by adding *-d or -ed* to the present: *skate, skated; walked, walked.*
- The simple past and the past participle of **irregular verbs** are not formed by adding *-ed* to the present: *ran, run.*

A **transitive verb** expresses an action that passes from a doer to a receiver. The receiver is the direct object of the verb: The dog *chewed* the bone.

A **verb phrase** is a group of words that does the work of a single verb. A verb phrase contains one or more **auxiliary verbs** (*is, are, has, have, will, can, could, do, would, should,* and so forth) and a **main verb**: She *had forgotten* her hat.

VOICE

In the **active voice,** the subject is the doer of the action: Betty *wrote* a poem.

In the **passive voice,** the subject is the receiver of the action. Only transitive verbs can be used in the passive voice: The poem *was written* by Betty.